A PORTRAIT OF
NEW ZEALAND

A PORTRAIT OF
NEW ZEALAND

PHOTOGRAPHS BY
ROBIN SMITH
WARREN JACOBS

TEXT BY
ERROL BRATHWAITE

KOWHAI PUBLISHING LTD.

CONTENTS

Active volcanoes, boiling mud and steaming geysers. Snow capped peaks and forest clad hills surrounding peaceful lakes. Clear trout-laden rivers cascading over waterfalls on their way to the coast.

Rich pastures raising the finest cattle, horses and sheep. Cultivated land producing abundant crops of fruit and vegetables. Vast pine plantation surrounding man-made hydro lakes. Proud cities built around reminders of our pioneer heritage.

Sheltered inlets dotted with islands — a boat owner's paradise, stormy headlands where oceans meet, beaches with golden and with black sands and harbours lined with crimson pohutukawa trees.

Glaciers that approach the sea, mountains eternally snow clad, alpine glades, tranquil 'bush' girt lakes, water falls and crystal clear rivers rushing seawards.

Plains patterned with shelter belts, tussock high country farms, verdant pastures and plantations, lakes made by man to harness energy, proud cities and towns lined with european trees and gardens.

Strange Moeraki boulders, Punakaiki's Pancake rocks, flooded volcanic craters, deep fiords, sandy bays, sheltered harbours and sounds, rocky headlands backed by mountains, river mouths and tidal estuaries.

NORTH ISLAND

Key to location of plates

8

SOUTH ISLAND

THE BEAUTY OF NEW ZEALAND'S

NORTH ISLAND

MOUNTAINS LAKES AND RIVERS — HOT AND COLD

The old-time Maoris used to say that the North Island of New Zealand was a fish, caught by the demi-god Maui from a canoe which became the South Island, with Stewart Island as its anchor stone. This sets the North Island atmosphere perfectly, because the hauling up of a fish of such prodigious size suggests of Homeric spectacle — and the North Island *is* spectacular. It suggests mystery, because how a people who knew no maps managed to perceive a fish-like shape of an island some 1,000km (600 miles) long is a mystery, the answer to which is buried deep in the lore of that mysterious people, in an island which abounds in awesome mystery.

The tale goes on to tell of how Maui's brothers, half crazed with hunger, leaped onto the monstrous fish and began to devour it raw, so that it is gouged and scarred, and its backbone is exposed, by their gnawings; and the picture thus conjured up is indeed a fair enough depiction of the North Island's highlands.

Visitors to New Zealand, coming first to the North Island, sometimes express wonder at the fact that they see no high alps, no mighty glaciers, though such features often fill New Zealand's commercial travel literature almost to the exclusion of all else. Yet few such comments reveal any sense of disappointment. On the contrary, the ecstatic visitor finds fresh evidence each day that what the North Island lacks in scenic grandeur, it makes up for amply in sheer spectacle. For this is a land in which the creative forces of the world are still awesomely at work. So are they in the South Island; but where the Southern Alps have been pushed up gradually, over aeons of time, by the infinitely ponderous movement of the plates of the earth's fractured crust, the highest mountains of the North Island have often leaped into being, or have suddenly disappeared, sometimes within remembered history, as the result or aftermath of violent explosions.

The same is true of many of its lakes and rivers. Where the South Island's alpine lakes have formed slowly in valleys carved by ice-age glacier, many North Island lakes began as massive subsidences due to earthquakes or subterranean upheavals.

Where pressure-folding has produced mountain ranges, the result stands for all to see — but the cause, being infinitely slow, is imperceptible; and some North Island ranges are still rising. So slow is the process, however,

Coromandel Range, near Coroglen.
The Coromandel Peninsula carries the high range which, in the vicinity of Whitianga, reaches to heights above 610m (2,000ft.). Exquisitely beautiful forest grows from the valleys where the ridges dovetail into one another, right to the tops, with tree fern and podocarps, and including stands of the lordly *kauri*. Alive with tui and fantail, grey warbler and the friendly native pigeon, they are traversed by roads which wind around their rocky spurs and frequently dive into deep, shady and now peaceful valleys, where men once milled the timber, and probed and dug for precious kauri gum.

13

Ruawaka Falls, Mangawhero River.
(above)
Today's main route from Raetihi to
Wanganui on the western coast
accompanies the Mangawhero River,
tributary to the scarcely larger
Whangaehu. The name means "Red
Stream," so called from the red algae
which coats rocks on its banks. Though it
runs for much of its length through tamed
pasture land, it still clutches to it a thin
fringe of native bush. The Ruawaka Falls,
dropping suddenly over the bush-screened
shelf, perhaps suggest ancient tragedies,
for their name means "Pit for Canoes."

Mount Egmont and Lake Mangamahoe.
(right)
Mount Egmont, for long thought to be an
extinct volcano, is now known to be
merely dormant. It once had a twin peak,
which shattered in some cataclysmic
explosion, and the tangle of forested hills
between the mountain and the city of New
Plymouth is its torn remnant. Lake
Mangamahoe's name suggests a
contradiction, because "Manga" means
"stream," and that is precisely what this
lake once was, before it was dammed to
form an artificial lake some 30-odd
hectares in area, supplying New Plymouth
with water and electricity.

that the Manawatu River, which rises on the eastern side of the island's
"backbone" mountain chain, flows out to the west coast, wearing its way
down as fast as the range rises, creating a deep gorge and separating the
mountain wall into two distinct and separate ranges, the Ruahines and the
Tararuas.

But where volcano, earthquake, rockfall and subsidence are the creators of
the landscape, the cause is usually still visible. On a clear day, from an
aeroplane, the volcanic fault-line which begins at the ferocious, Etna-like
volcano out in the Bay of Plenty, called White Island, may be easily discerned
in the rift-valleys, and in the long chain of volcanic peaks, steaming lakes,
fumarols and active volcanoes that stretches diagonally from the Bay of
Plenty coast to the central volcanic plateau. The force which shaped this
landscape, which collapsed it, tossed it, tumbled and tangled it, is still there,
still visible, still working, still smoking and steaming and filling the air with
its sulphurous breath.

The largest visible subsidence area is right in the middle of the island. The
water of a major river and a dozen other sizeable streams flow into it, to form
New Zealand's largest lake, Lake Taupo, 41km (25 miles) long and up to
27km (17 miles) wide, with a total area of 238 square miles. The lake has,
flowing into it at one end and out of it at the other, New Zealand's longest
river, the Waikato, 434km (270 miles) long.

The North Island's mountains do not compare in size with those of the
Southern Alps. Highest is Mount Ruapehu, 2,797m (9,175ft), about 58th in
the list of New Zealand's highest mountains, yet quite high enough to have
snow on its peak all year round; and what it lacks in height, it makes up for
in wonder, with its crater lake steaming hot, though surrounded by ice and
snow to its very edge.

North Islanders, like South Islanders, seldom live out of sight of the
mountains, though there are some exceptions. In Northland there are steep,

14

Huka Falls, Waikato River. (above)
The young Waikato River slips down
from the level land through which it
comes away from Lake Taupo, only to
slip, as it were, on a sloping, rocky scarp
which has been split by some gigantic
earthquake. For some 200m (656ft), it
slides down, ever more narrowly confined,
ever gathering momentum, bullying its
way past great boulders, plucking at
riverside vegetation, until it makes its ten-
metre leap over the Huka Falls in an
earth-shaking display of power.

rugged hills which, in some older lands, would doubtless be labelled
"mountain," but which are not exceptionally high in rugged New Zealand,
and are never snow-crowned, but have forested tops. But in almost every
other part of New Zealand's North Island, mountains dominate the skyline,
along a great chain which runs from Mt. Hikurangi, 1,709m (5,606ft),
claimed to be the first peak in New Zealand to be lit by the rising sun — a
claim it shares with Mt. Cook, according to some authorities. The mountain
chain runs down through the Raukumara Range, the Kaweka Range, the
tangled massif of the Kaimanawas, the curving wall of the Ruahine Range,
and the steep Tararuas. Rising in a long curve southward from the base of
the Coromandel Peninsula is the Kaimai Range, forested to its tops; and
branching from the edge of the volcanic plateau is a vast area of crumpled
high-country, densely forested, which rises at its western edge up to the
slopes of Mount Egmont, 2,518m (8,260ft), sometimes referred to as New
Zealand's Fujiyama, a dormant volcano on the West Cape.

Though they are not as high or as grand as the Southern Alps, it is,
nevertheless, amongst the mountains of the North Island that the largest,
most beautiful lakes lie; and from their bush-clad flanks flow great rivers,

16

Tongariro River. (above)
The Tongariro River rises, as might be expected, on the eastern flanks of Mount Ruapehu, in Tongariro National Park. It is, somewhat confusingly, known as the Upper Waikato from its source to where it is joined by the Waihohonu Stream, though from this point it is known officially as the Tongariro River to where it flows into Lake Taupo. There is less confusion, however, in its reputation as a trout stream. Anglers world wide consider it without a doubt the best fishing river in New Zealand, and one of the finest in the world.

Trout, Rainbow Springs, Rotorua. (left)
Rainbow Springs, (and the nearby Fairy Springs), are famous for the crystal clarity of the water, and the fat trout which inhabit them. A path wanders alongside the stream, slightly below it, and underwater viewing windows allow visitors to observe the giant (and captive) brown trout closely. Welling springs uplift grains of white pumice and black obsidian — for this is on the volcanic fault line — which colour the water a lovely shade of blue.

17

Mangawhero River, Near Ohakune.
(previous page right)
From the south-western slopes of Mount Ruapehu, the Mangawhero River fights its way over a boulder-strewn, scrub-covered, volcanic landscape, running into heavy bush as it sweeps past Raetihi and Ohakune, accompanying the Parapara Gorge route between Raetihi and Wanganui, and thrusting at last into the Whangaehu River. Even in the peaceful calm of the forest, away from the rifted landscape about its parent mountain, it surges forward with impatient power, crashing past ancient, mossy boulders, and overwhelming ridges and upthrustings of rock.

Mount Ruapehu, Evening Light.
(previous page above left)
The sun, setting in a blaze of rose-coloured glory, bathes the broken hulk of Mount Ruapehu in a pink glow, and touches with red the snow-patched tussock in the grim desert of pumice soil at the volcano's feet. The biggest of three volcanic mountains on the central plateau, Ruapehu stands 2,797m (9,175ft), a broken, truncated cone which was once much higher. It cradles in its crater a steaming lake, acid-tinged and sulphurous.

Rainbow Falls, Keri Keri, Bay of Islands
(previous page below left)
On the lower reaches of the Keri Keri River, about 5km (3 miles) upstream from where it runs out into its sheltered inlet, the placid, narrow, meandering stream takes a sudden dramatic plunge over a rocky ledge. The falls usually have a fragile veil of spray which, when it catches the sun's rays, paints a rainbow across the basin into which the water falls. The white water, the rainbow and the surrounding filigree of greenery are an exquisite little cameo in a landscape where even the clay in the roadside banks is tinted a delicate rose pink; for this is, or was, a volcanic countryside.

Huka Rapids. (above)
Some 200m upstream from the Huka Falls, the Waikato River slips on an inclined shelf of rock and slides down, dropping about 9m in that distance. It gathers speed as it races down to the head of the Huka Falls, clutching at the sides of the cleft, crashing over boulders, twisting, turning, tumbling, never in the whole of its length displaying more power than it does here, yet confined to a width of a mere 15-16m. The name, Huka, means "Foam," and, like many Maori names, is descriptive, especially where the river plunges at last some 12m a maelstrom of turquoise-green and white foam.

The Wairoa River. (right)
The Wairoa River is a mere 80km in length, yet within that short compass it is one of the most complex river systems in New Zealand. The Waiau River, flowing south-eastwards, is swelled by the waters of the Waikare-taheke, which drains Lake Waikaremoana, and joins the Wairoa near Frasertown. The Ruakituri and Hangaroa Rivers run down from the north-west into the Wairoa, and the Mangapoike Stream joins it from the north-east. The result is a broad, smoothly flowing river watering a rich, alluvial countryside around the town of Wairoa. Navigable for about 23km (15 miles) from its mouth, it made of the little town a minor port in the days before the road and rail reached it from north and south.

deep and frequently navigable, and not gravel-choked like the rivers of Canterbury. On some North Island mountains are skifields which are famous world-wide, or which are relatively new and growing fast in popularity. On some are resorts highly regarded for their exquisite scenery. Some cradle lakeside resorts on their flanks. Others smoulder and spit and rumble menacingly, and trail their skirts in weird areas of boiling mud, geysers, silica terraces and sulphurous steam. And all of them have a brooding quality, an air of dark secrecy that can be a little daunting; yet all, when they are approached and their territory entered, open up their treasures readily, and are captivating in the extreme.

Perhaps it suffices to say that the North Island's mountains, lakes, rivers and thermal areas have a shape, an aspect, an atmosphere all of their own — and they are unsurpassed anywhere for sheer, breathtaking beauty.

Taken all in all, there is less nostalgia apparent in the North Island. There are some attempts to reproduce something of a homeland which the first settlers had left to come here, but nothing to compare with, say, the almost aggressive Englishness of Christchurch or the equally determined Scottishness of Dunedin. Always there is a frank, if enforced, acknowledgement of the fact, forced upon them at every turn, that they and their culture were a transplant. You see it in public gardens, like the Lady Norwood Rose Garden in Wellington, where the dainty flowers, in their straight and formal rows, bloom against a background of cheerfully unkempt native shrubs and trees. You are made aware of it by towns which were originally named after English localities, but which, in time, reverted to the Maori name for the place, even though the streets, in good English fashion, retain the names of past aldermen, famous generals and Empire dignitaries.

21

Panekiri Bluff, Lake Waikaremoana. (above)
The Panekiri Range rises up on one side of Lake Waikaremoana, with peaks of over 1,067m (3,500ft) high, running north-eastwards to terminate in the high and dramatic bluff that drops into the lake. This beautiful, star-shaped lake lies in the Urewera Highlands at an altitude of 614m (2,015ft) above sea level, surrounded by densely forested mountains. Formed by an ancient rock-fall which blocked the path of the Waikare-taheke River, it is some 21 square miles in area, with depths of up to 247m (846ft), and is fed by many mountain streams which come down to the lake, often over exquisite waterfalls.

Green Lake, Rotorua. (right)
In the twisted, fragmented, rumpled landscape south of Rotorua, on the wonderfully scenic road that goes to Buried Village and Lake Tarawera, lie the twin lakes, Green Lake and Blue Lake, separated by a narrow neck of tree-covered land, and named for the colour of their waters. The Maori name for Green Lake is Rotokakahi, which means "Lake of the Kakahi" (Fresh-water Mussel), which the Maoris found to be particularly abundant in its clear waters.

22

Mount Ngauruhoe and Whakapapanui Stream. (above)
Of the trio of volcanoes, Ruapehu, Ngauruhoe and Tongariro, that rise out of the central volcanic plateau, Mount Ngauruhoe is the most symmetrical. Rising 2,291m (7,515ft), it emerges from a shattered tangle of craters and rifts of which it has gradually become the dominant feature, the next highest eminence in the complex being Tongariro, 1,968m (6,458ft). From the flanks of Ruapehu, the largest and southernmost peak, flows the Whakapapanui Stream, running down across a scrub-and-pumice landscape to join the Whakapapa, an upper tributary of the Wanganui River. On its way down, it foams over the Tawhai Falls, the Mahuia Rapids and the Toakakura and Matariki Falls.

It is one of the fascinations of the North Island that the thing worked both ways. The Maori Queen, Te Ata-i-rangi-Kaahu, lives in her palace at Ngaruawahia — a palace which is simply a largish European bungalow with carved wooden panels instead of weatherboard, and bargeboards embellished with fine Maori carving. And at Ohinemutu, on the shores of Lake Rotorua, a bust of Queen Victoria stands upon a pedestal, protected from the elements by a little wooden house with decorated bargeboards and carved pillars.

The cultures never really fused. For long, many people of both races told themselves and each other that they had; but it is not so, and the realisation is dawning that it is better that it is not so. As each race acknowledges its difference, respect and appreciation can go hand-in-hand and this is beginning to happen. As it does, the fascination of the North Island will grow, and what is at present an ingredient in its difference will become one of its principal attractions.

Mud Pool. (above)
Mud pools are a source of almost endless
fascination. The mud gurgles and slurps
like hot porridge in a pot; and one such
pool, at Whakarewarewa, is known as the
Frog Pond, because gouts of mud, thrown
from bursting mud bubbles, seem to hop
across the surface like small silver frogs, a
phenomenon which occurs after rain,
when the mud is less viscous.

*Mt. Ngauruhoe, Tongariro National Park.
(right)*
Mt. Ngauruhoe is thought to have been
formed about 2,500 years ago, no great age
for a volcano. In continuous eruption, it
mostly emits gas in the form of steam, but
from time to time it becomes somewhat
more violent and belches forth ash.
Geological records show that it spilled
forth red hot lava in 1949, and again in
1954, and in contrast to the ash explosions
which last for a short time, from mere
minutes to a few days, the lava
outpourings are apt to go on for months.
There are walking tracks in the vicinity of
the cone, but it is necessary to watch
closely for any sign of increasing activity,
and to get clear away as quickly as
possible when such signs are noticed.

24

Tarawera Volcanic Rent. (above left)
In the early morning of June 10th, 1886, at precisely 12.30am, a series of earthquakes began, increasing in violence for an hour. Then, at 1.30am, a small explosion occurred on the north-eastern end of the mountain. At 1.45am, a horrendous roar burst from the vicinity of Ruawahia Peak, and a vast black column, shot with the glowing red of hot rocks, rocketed skywards. Twenty minutes later, with an even more deafening roar, the south-eastern end of the mountain burst open, throwing up a cloud which was seen from Gisborne, some 140km (87 miles) away, and estimated to be 10km (6 miles) high. It was followed by explosion after explosion, vast, bellowing holocausts which were heard at distant Coromandel, over 161km (100 miles) distant, as a chain of craters 19km (12 miles) long ripped the mountain apart. An estimated 155 people, two Maori settlements and the European village of Te Wairoa were destroyed.

Terrace Formations, Whakarewarewa. (below left)
A recurring feature of the thermal areas are the often dazzling terraces of silvery-white silica, streaked in many places by deposits of other minerals. The most famous terrace formation for many years was that known as the Pink and White Terraces in the Rotomahana Basin, destroyed by the eruption of Mount Tarawera in 1886.

Steaming Cliffs, Lake Rotomahana. (above right)
The Rotomahana Basin, with its exquisite Pink and White Terraces, was an internationally famous tourist attraction, and one of the natural wonders of the world, in the latter half of last century. The eruption of Mount Tarawera destroyed it and created here a lake, which itself has become a tourist attraction, with its large areas of boiling water bubbling up in the midst of an expanse of ordinarily cold water. This, with the Steaming Cliffs, leave no doubt that the lake fills what is to all intents and purposes a large volanic rift or crater.

Mt. Ngauruhoe Erupting. (below right)
The smoke clings to, and rolls down the flanks of, the perfect cone, and a powdering of fine ash may spread across the country as far as Hawkes Bay to the east, across the Kaiwekas, or to the Tasman Sea coast, to colour the sunsets for days at a time. When it occurs in winter, the snowy peaks are smeared and blotched with grey. But this is not a particularly violent eruption, and there is no glowing magma being tossed high into the sky, nor any avalanches of ash and hot rock bounding down the mountainside. This eruption is merely one of the mountain's periodic grumblings.

Craters of the Moon. Wairakei. (above)
The Wairakei Valley is an area slightly to
the north of Taupo, a place of steaming
pools and silica terraces, which once held
a number of spectacular geysers. Today,
due to the tapping of the underground
steam for the Wairakei Geothermal Power
scheme, they no longer erupt. But a new
area has been opened up — the Craters of
the Moon, which includes steaming,
bubbling pits, and the famed Karapiti
Blowhole, a fumarole of considerable
activity, as an indication of the colossal
power which seethes and fumes beneath
the trembling ground.

*Wairakei Geothermal Power Station.
(right)*
Steam bores, sunk into the sub-surface
cauldron of the Wairakei Valley, tap the
vast energy source of the thermal region,
and feed the high-pressure steam to
turbines in a power station which has a
load capacity of some 192 megawatts,
about 5% of the country's total
consumption. The generators are housed
in a unique building designed to stand
earthquake shocks without the turbine
chamber floors being tilted or disturbed
unduly.

Pohutu Geyser, Whakarewarewa. (left)
Whakarewarewa, perhaps the best known
of the Rotorua thermal parks, is on the
southern edge of Rotorua city. More than
500 hot springs boil here with varying
degrees of violence, and a Maori village
spreads around its eastern edge, the
inhabitants using the hot pools for
cooking and other domestic purposes. The
area is a mere 1km (½ mile) long by 500m
(546 yards) wide. The finest spectacle is
the famous Pohutu Geyser, which hurls
a jet of steaming water to heights of 18m
(60ft) and more.

White Island. (above right)
Grumbling and steaming 50km (30 miles)
off the Bay of Plenty coast, White Island
is a steadily active volcano. Privately
owned, it can be visited by boat in calm
weather, permission having first been
obtained; and recently it has become
possible to visit it by helicopter. But it is
a dangerous place, with its little lakes of
acid and its acid mud and occasional
whiffs of toxic fumes. The floor of the
crater is below sea level.

Champagne Pool, Waiotapu. (below right)
About 30km (18½ miles) south of Rotorua,
the Waiotapu Reserve possesses some of
the finest thermal activity spectacles in the
area, including the outstanding Lady
Knox Geyser, the Frying Pan, Echo Lake,
Chromatopsia Terraces, the Explosion
Craters, Alum Cliffs, Venus Baths,
Primrose Terrace and the impressive hot
waterfall. The Champagne Pool is a
sizeable lake which, when a handful of
sand is tossed into it, bubbles like
champagne, which it also approximates
in colour.

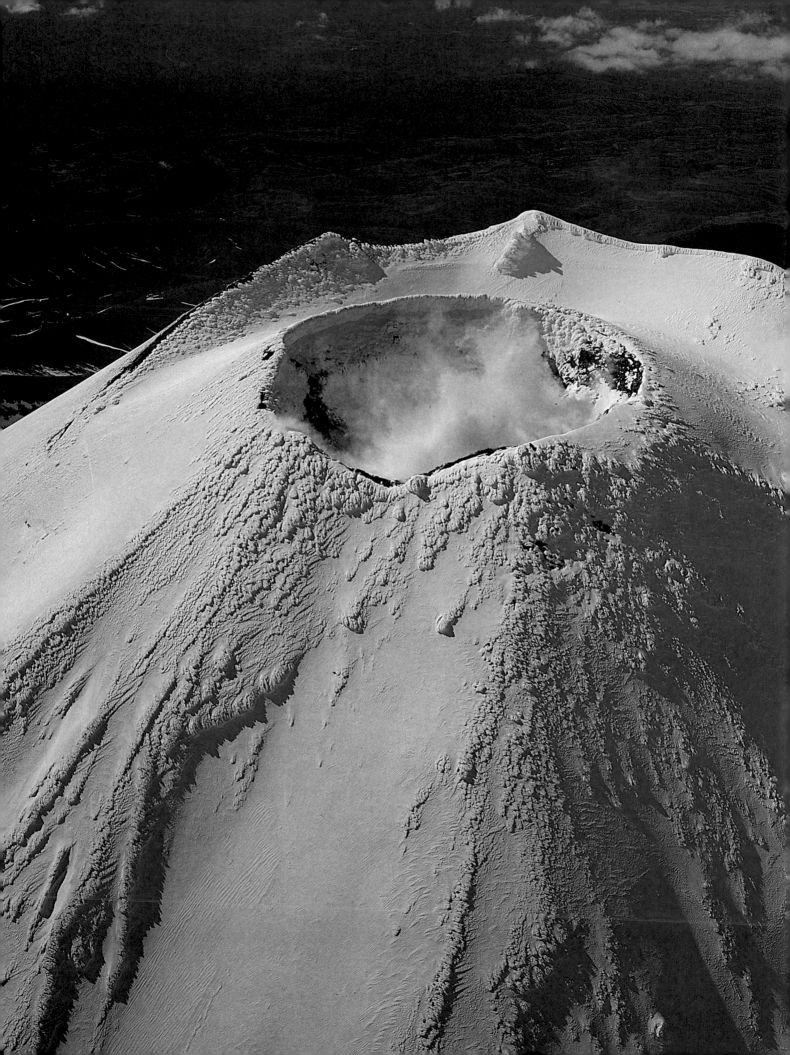

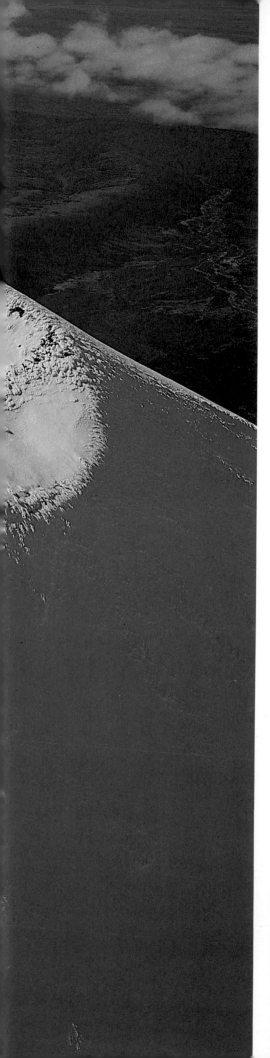

The Summit, Mount Ngauruhoe. (left)
The fascinating double crater at the top of
Mount Ngauruhoe's cone is a clue to the
way in which the mountain itself grew.
The lovely cone rises out of the shattered,
multi-cratered flank of Mount Tongariro,
a vent which clearly has developed into a
distinct and separate mountain. On its
own top, a creater within the original
crater has opened up, forming a cone
upon the original cone. Ngauruhoe has
grown large and distinct enough to be
considered a separate mountain only
within the last century.

*Thermal Activity, Tikitere, (Hell's Gate),
Rotorua. (below)*
Between Lakes Rotorua and Rotoiti is
Tikitere, named "Hell's Gate" for extra —
and hardly necessary — dramatic effect.
This is the most active of the thermal
areas, a series of cauldrons of boiling
water, seething mud, fumaroles and
sulphurous steam, where the ground
trembles with the pent-up power beneath
the surface.

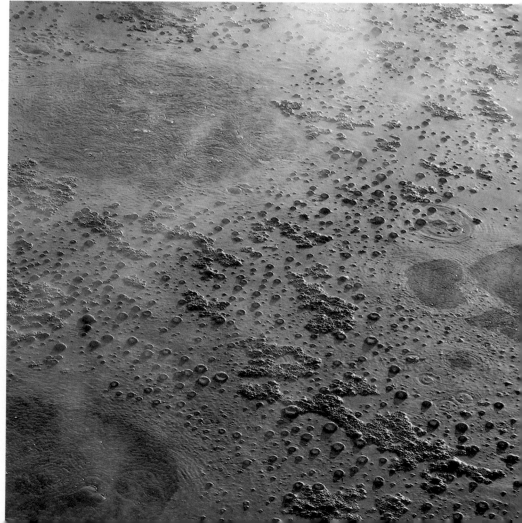

Mokau River and Lake Waikaremoana. (above left)
Rising on the slopes of the bush-clad mountain, Pukepuke, (which translates oddly as Hill Hill), to the north of Lake Waikareiti, the Mokau River is a swift-flowing mountain stream which flows into the Mokau Arm of Lake Waikaremoana. Near the point of entry, it drops over a great buttress of rock to form the Mokau Falls, one of the many delightful cascades in the area.

Waikari River, Hawkes Bay. (below left)
Almost half way between Napier and Wairoa, perhaps 8km (5 miles) inland from the centre of Hawke's Bay horseshoe curve, the settlement of Putorino (the name is that of a Maori flute), spreads along the banks of the Waikari River. Maori legend says that it is named from an incident in the travels of their ancient explorer, Paoa, when his dog kept on digging until he found water. But the story does the lovely stream less than justice. It is a picturesque water, where native bush and Old World willow combine to shade its pools, in a valley of great beauty.

Kauri Tree Near Russell, Bay of Islands. (right)
Not the least of the attractions of the Northland bays and harbours for the old-time whalers and traders was the seemingly infinite supply of kauri trees. The kauri was huge and straight-grained. Its trunk, branchless for many metres, was tough and wonderfully durable, and made magnificent masts and spars. But it takes something like a thousand years to reach the height and maturity they preferred, and the timber-takers nearly cut it to extinction. Today it is rigidly protected.

Kowhai Flowers.
The kowhai tree is, generally speaking, a forest-edge tree, starting life as a tiny shrub seedling in the protecting shade of the tall trees. Related to the broom, it is much more spindly, and usually much taller, with great pendant clusters of golden flowers in season. A legume, it is part of the same plant family as the similar, though scarlet, kaka-beak, and, perhaps surprisingly, the common or garden pea.

Papakorito Falls, Waikaremoana. (right)
The Aniwaniwa (Rainbow) Stream comes down from the bush-clad tops, tumbling over the steep slopes of the Urewera Highlands, leaping over perpendicular walls of rock, to the beautiful Whanganui-a-parua Arm of Lake Waikaremoana. The best-known cascade on this rushing stream is that known as Aniwaniwa Falls; but scarcely less beautiful, though smaller, is the waterfall known as Papakorito Fall, where a level reach of the river suddenly tumbles in three dramatic tiers down into a tree-shaded basin.

Lake Tarawera. (above)
The lovely way which winds past the Blue and Green Lakes, and slips discreetly past Te Wairoa, the Buried Village, dips down at last to a bush-fringed shore, on which there is a cavern containing the ancient rock drawings of the Maori. And from this shore there stretches a large and beautiful lake, at the far end of which rises a truncated cone, dreadfully shattered and gashed. The lake is Lake Tarawera, and the broken mountain is Mount Tarawera, which, on June 10th, 1886, exploded with devastating force, burying the little village of Te Wairoa and other lakeside settlements beneath many metres of hot ash and pumice. The surrounding countryside was ravaged and tumbled by the accompanying earthquakes, and there was a great loss of life. Today, the regenerated forest and the sheltering, enclosing hills make it difficult to imagine the devastation of that night of terror.

38

Acacia Bay, Lake Taupo. (left)
Boats drawn up on a beach strewn with
chunks of the strange, light, porous,
floating rock called pumice, the launches
and yachts riding at anchor in the cove, or
leaning like small, white pyramids far out
on the lake, and the prospect of a distant
shore, create a scene which belongs to the
seacoast, rather than to the centre of a
rugged island, some 369m (1,211ft) above
sea level. But that's what Lake Taupo is
— an inland sea which, before the roads
were pushed through, was plied by at
least one steamer, using the lake as the
main highway to Rotorua.

*Sunset Over Lake Taupo and the
Volcanoes. (above)*
Lake Taupo is New Zealand's largest lake.
Some 41km (25 miles) in length, 27km (17
miles) wide at its widest point, it lies in a
great subsidence. A water of many moods,
it can be sparklingly inviting when the
summer sun is high and the dazzling
pumice beaches are hot underfoot; and it
can whip up into sudden rages when the
winds sweep down over the volcanic
plateau and stir its waters into a
dangerous turbulence. But within an hour
of such a storm, when the wind dies at
evening, it can lie peacefully again in a
flat and dreamy calm, reflecting the sunset
light from a washed sky.

Mokau River, near Te Kuiti, King Country. (above)
The placid stream which winds delightfully through meadows and between high limestone bluffs grows as it meanders towards the Tasman Sea coast to become one of New Zealand's finest waterways, yet one which, today, is probably the least known navigable stream in New Zealand. Just over 125km (75 miles) in length, its lower reaches flow between cliffs crowned spectacularly with forest, as fine as anything on the Wanganui River; and until the late 1920s or early 1930s, regular sea-going traffic plied upstream for some 38km (23 miles) to the one-time port of Mokau, and its coal mines.

Glow-Worm Grotto, Waitomo Caves. (right)
Down the centre of the North Island, and for some distance through the South Island, are vast reefs of limestone, and in the Waitomo District of the King Country these are riddled with underground streams. Best known are the Waitomo Caves, a group of caverns known individually as Waitomo Cave, Ruakuri Cave and Aranui Cave. The glow-worms are the larval form of an insect, *(Boletophila luminosa)*, which suspend themselves from the cave roof by a sticky thread which traps insects. Viewed from a boat in pitch darkness, the glow-worms appear as vast constellations of blue-white lights, unforgettably beautiful.

Wanganui River, from Gentle Annie Hill.
(above)
The Wanganui River has been called the
Rhine of New Zealand. Its valley is indeed
gentle with farms and dark with forests, it
is navigable, (though seldom navigated by
anything larger than a jet boat, today),
and was once a main highway to the
interior. It even had the occasional
fighting *pa* perched like a robber baron's
castle on crags overlooking the stream.
Two hundred and twenty-six kilometres
(140 miles) long, its terminal port for its
once considerable traffic was Taumaranui,
a hundred river-miles (162km) and 90
rapids inland from the river's broad
mouth on the Tasman Sea coast.

Lake Tutira, Hawkes Bay. (right)
On the main road between Napier and
Wairoa, Lake Tutira lies in a green basin,
bush and willow fringed, the haunt of a
wide variety of native and introduced
waterfowl, for which it is a sanctuary. In
the 1930s, the land about the lake was
extensively planted with trees in a
successful effort to halt erosion. Lake
Tutira is separated from its smaller
neighbour, Lake Waikopiro, by a narrow
tongue of land; and both, ultimately,
drain through a narrow rift into the
Waikoau River.

Lake Waikaremoana Sunset. (above)
Considered by many to be, (with the
South Island's Lake Manapouri), one of
New Zealand's two most beautiful lakes,
Waikaremoana is an intricate stretch of
waterways, with inlets and islands and
coves of a Garden-of-Eden-like beauty. It
has a range of moods, as is indicated by
its name, which means "Sea of Turbulent
Waters," (not "Rippling Waters," as it is
usually rendered). At its 614m (2,014ft)
altitude, bluffs stand sharply forth and
forested crests are silhouetted cleanly in
the crystal-clear air, constant reminders
that this magnificent lake is situated in
the midst of romantically wild highlands
— never more so than at evening, when
the tops are black against a spectacular
sky.

43

Crater Lake, Mount Ruapehu. (left)
Ruapehu is still very much an active volcano, as is Ngauruhoe's symmetrical cone, rising in the near distance. But Ruapehu, between eruptions, cradles in its snow-bound crater a sulphurous, somewhat acid lake of steaming water, which periodically disappears, to be replaced by a sullen, spitting, fuming hole which belches forth mud and ash.

Mount Ruapehu (above)
From the vicinity of Ohakune, 25km (15 miles) to the south-west, Mount Ruapehu stands revealed as an awesomely broken cone, snow-covered, with broad faces providing excellent ski fields. The longest established fields, and those best known internationally, are reached from Chateau Tongariro, at the foot of that long, rough slope beyond the flat, bush-covered spur. But on the near side of the mountain, comparatively newly developed fields, reached by road from Ohakune, are growing steadily in popularity.

MAN'S HAND THE NORTH ISLAND

Even before the advent of the European, the Maori had made his unmistakeable mark on the landscape. The North Island abounds in hills which, in tribal days, were stragtegically or tactically important; and these remain ridged with entrenchments, and dented with pits which once held food stores and sunken *whares*. There is, too, at least one rivermouth silted up as the result of their campaigning, when a whole tribe's sea-going vessels sank at anchor in the estuary. Here and there, ancient palisade posts mark the site of an old *pa*; and there are still, amongst the fern and scrub of a silent countryside, earthen forts designed to cope with bullet and cannon shell. Little else remains of the Maoris' pre-European or early-European existence; because these hardy Polynesians, though they planted often extensive gardens, and built towns with populations of up to ten thousand souls, lived with, not against, nature. They followed nature's moods and seasons, moving from cultivation to bird-spearing forest, to fishing grounds, to eeling swamps, and they took from forest, river, lake and sea only as much as they needed. The greater part of their rigidly upheld law lay in the field of conservations six hundred years before the *pakeha*, the white stranger, ever thought of it. Therefore, it is the pakeha who has wrought the greatest changes, in a brief century and a half, stripping thousands of square miles of jungle from the hills and turning them into pasture, garden, township, city and exotic forest, with road and rail, airport and harbour to link town with town and farm with farm, and tying New Zealand into the vast network of the world's commerce and communication.

This much may be said of both the North and South Islands; yet there remains a discernible difference between the impression made by the North Island settlers on their environment and the mark made by the South Island pioneers.

North Island pioneers worked no less diligently than their South Island counterparts, but their task was immeasureably harder. The two or three planned settlement schemes were less well organised, perhaps because they were generally earlier than the South Island schemes, and the colonists and the scheme's organisers had less knowledge of the conditions they would have to contend with. Further, there was a larger Maori population in the North Island, and a clash was inevitable. It came, it grew and it dragged on through nearly forty years of intermittent and bitter warfare. Settlers saw the

Pastoral Scene near Waipukurau, Hawkes Bay.
Limestone-skeletoned hills, rolling and gentle, provide lush pasturage for sheep, in central Hawkes Bay. The country is well watered by myriad small creeks and streams, tributaries of the Tuki-tuki River. Where once there was much forest, and swamp-filled valleys, the settlers created an almost European landscape of willow and poplar and pine, with small, neat towns, and hillsides ridged and terraced by the feet of a million sheep. This is some of the richest pastoral land in New Zealand.

Wairarapa Pastoral Scene near Masterton. (above)
Masterton, at the northern end of the Wairarapa Plain, is the administrative centre for Wairarapa County, one of the three southernmost counties in the Wairarapa District, which between them graze over two million sheep. Between Masterton and the coast, the plain gives way to rolling hills and twisting valleys, well watered and fertile, some of the finest pastoral country in New Zealand.

Farmlands, Tarawera. (right)
The farmlands of Tarawera are relatively new. A volcanic countryside, once a wasteland of pumice- and ash-covered soil, it lay for long beneath a rank burden of fern and scrub with, here and there, patches of regenerated forest. It was discovered, however, that the land was remarkably fertile, and in the past thirty to forty years, much of it has been transformed into highly productive grazing land. The task has been no easy one, even so, for this is a relatively high rainfall area with a climate on the warm side of temperate, in which a paddock left ungrazed for a few weeks can rapidly revert to a bracken-covered wilderness.

fruits of their prodigious labours go up in the smoke and flames of sudden raid and pitched battle.

And then again, communities were born and grew up in isolation one from another. In the South Island, communities tended to grow at the end of each road or railway as it stretched forth from the original settlement, over plain and river and coastal hill. In the North Island, settlers were landed by boat in little coastal enclaves which were separated from other such enclaves by hundreds of miles of dense forest, rugged terrain and, often, hostile tribes; and they remained isolated until road and rail pushed through to them. One of the greatest marks of man's occupation, then, consists of engineering feats, like the Raurimu Spiral, where all but insurmountable difficulties of terrain were overcome.

There are, of course, other marks. The towns, often enough, are less well planned than those of the South Island, largely because, in a hostile environment, settlers' houses huddled closely together for security and comfort; and, also, every quarter acre that was pegged out for a family dwelling had to be hacked out, often enough, from the close-crowding bush; so streets, created at the expense of vast and herculean effort, are often narrower than their South Island counterparts.

Roads, pushed through wildernesses so that soldiers could move quickly from point to point, were as wide as was necessary to accommodate a train of artillery or a column of infantry; and they tended to stick close to the valley floors, save where swamps and rivers forced them to climb higher, in which case they followed the crests of ridges at gradients practical for bullock waggons. There are, today, motorways on main trunk routes and some secondary systems, where gradients have since been made easier, and bends which were dangerous for modern, high-speed traffic eased or straightened; but the country roads still follow the bullock and pack-horse trails, and though sealed, are still frequently anachronistically narrow.

Auckland City. (far left)
Auckland, once the seat of Government, has long been New Zealand's largest, most cosmopolitan city. With its tall, white high-rises in the city centre, its sprawling suburbs scrambling over a scatter of ancient volcanic cones, its sparkling, blue, beautiful harbour whose name, Waitemata, is said to mean "Sparkling Waters," (but more probably is short for Wai-te-matatuhua, meaning "Water as Smooth as Obsidian"), the city is a vital, lively, well-favoured home for over half a million New Zealanders.

Auckland and Harbour. (above left)
Aucklanders have a much more outdoors life-style than the people of most other New Zealand centres, and their outdoors activity centres around the lovely Waitemata Harbour, which wanders up long inlets, is spanned by a great bridge, and is brooded over by the cone of Rangitoto, a 269m (854ft) volcano, extinct but of recent enough activity to be a barren place of jagged lava and scoria, and stunted, stubborn plant life.

Parnell Village Street, Auckland. (below left)
In one of Auckland's oldest suburbs, a man named Les Harvey, (who detests high-rise buildings, regarding them as ant heaps in which it is wrong to incarcerate people), collected as many of the delightful old Victorian shops and wooden buildings as he could find, and created a people-sized shopping centre which recaptures the intimate magic of old-style shops, with their shady verandas and many-paned windows.

Dairy Herd Near Carterton, Wairarapa.
(below)
The rolling country of the northern
Wairarapa gives way, in the south to a
wide and slightly undulating plain before
sinking down on its western side into the
depression filled by Lake Wairarapa and
Lake Ferry, and rising again in the east to
terminate in high bluffs overlooking Cook
Strait. This relatively flat land is fine
dairying country, where dairy herds such
as these Jersey cows browse in a tree-
dotted lushly green landscape.

Landscape Between New Plymouth and
Mount Egmont. (right)
The land about the northern skirts of
Mount Egmont is a crumpled, steep tract,
heavily forested a mere century ago, and
still carrying areas of dense bush on the
actual flank of the mountain, and on the
shattered remains of what was once
Egmont's twin volcano.

*The Kaukatea Valley, near Wanganui.
(left)*
The Kaukatea Valley still wears patches of
the native bush which once covered much
of this landscape, and has now been
replaced with isolated stands of Old
World poplar and conifers. But the
cabbage tree still dots the paddocks. A
member of the lily family, its trunk is
useless for building, composed as it is of
tightly packed, coarse fibres; yet the
pioneers found the tree valuable. The
hearts of its palm-like foliage can be
cooked like cabbage — Captain Cook
made use of it as a kind of sauerkraut, to
protect his crew against scurvy — and
very tender and palatable it is.

*The Waiau Valley, near Wairoa, Hawkes
Bay. (above)*
From a number of small streams flowing
down from the Urewera Highlands
towards Lake Waikaremoana, the Waiau
River is formed. It does not flow into the
lake, but trends eastwards and flows down
to join the Wairoa about 16km (10 miles)
from the little hamlet and one-time
garrison post of Frasertown. A wild
stretch of water in its upper reaches,
flowing through wild country, it gentles
as the countryside softens, and presently
drifts peaceably through a green and
pleasant valley shaded with oak and elm
and willow. Yet even here the fern can
spring quickly from the roadside verges, and the forested hills are still in plain
view. So the Waiau Valley makes a sort of
frontier, where cultivation and imposed
order meets the primeval jungle of the
Urewera hills.

Fishing Fleet, Gisborne. (above)
Though the bay in which Gisborne sits is
called Poverty Bay, the district is a region
of rich productivity. Fine wines are grown
around Gisborne, and much of the
countryside is highly favoured
pastureland. Fishing is very much a
minor industry, yet a small off-shore
fishing fleet operates out of the
rivermouth harbour, which can
accommodate ships of up to 3,200 tons.
The Waimata and Taruheru Rivers join a
little distance upstream from the coast,
near the centre of the city, to form the
Turanganui River, which is thus the
shortest river in New Zealand.

*Maraetai Dam and Mangakino.
(right)*
One of several hydro-electric dams on the
Waikato River, the Maraetai Dam, 87m
(285ft) high, has formed a lake nearly 600
hectares (1,100 acres) in extent and 76m
(250ft) deep. Mangakino township was
established in the late 1940s for the
accommodation of construction workers
on the Maraetai dam and two other hydro
dams, Whakamaru and Atiamuri,
upstream. When construction was
complete, the township remained as a
market and administrative centre for a
land settlement scheme which turned the
scrub and fern wastelands into highly
productive farmland.

Wylie Cottage, Gisborne. (left)
The pioneers seldom had time for the building of large houses, in the wild areas around Poverty Bay. Nevertheless, many of the pioneer houses remaining are gems of graceful and dignified architcture, though built in a way which ensured comparative ease and speed of erection. This beautiful little house is a straightforward, uncomplicated rectangle, with a roofed veranda across the front and a lean-to extension at the rear. The upper floor is lit by windows under the gables, and a small dormer. Weatherboarding timbers are laid perpendicularly, not overlapping but with weatherproofing cleats over the joins. The roof is shingled. Overall, it is a delightful little home, and one which would be popular and convenient today.

The Treaty House, Waitangi. (below)
The official name for this house was The Residency, for it was the dwelling, office and court of the Lieutenant Governor. Designed by the official Colonial Architect, it has a Georgian cleanness and simplicity. Its rooms are well proportioned and spacious, and its French windows look out across a sweep of lawn to the Bay of Islands. On the lawn, the Treaty of Waitangi was presented and signed in 1840.

Landscape Near Taumaranui. (previous page)

The King Country is a region of contrasts — of green sheep runs on ruggedly steep country, of ploughed fields and wrapped around surprisingly precipitous faces, of sudden marches of dark forest enwrapping willow-shaded brooks in valley meadows — and Taumaranui, a bustling township of around 5,000 people, deep in the King Country hills — until forty years ago a port, over sixty river miles from the sea!

Wanganui from Papaiti Hill. (above)

Wanganui, at the mouth of the Wanganui River, was one of New Zealand's earliest settlements, and is, today, one of the country's most picturesque cities. Renowned for delightful public parks and gardens, for its beautiful homes and, most of all, for its river, it possesses a number of architectural splendours and landmarks, such as the lookout tower, (seen on the far horizon), on Durie Hill, a castelated stone tower into which an elevator ascends from the foot of the hill.

Wellington City at Night. (above)
Wellington, the nation's Capital, is superbly situated about an immense, almost land-locked harbour, of which nineteenth century commentators used to say that it would shelter all the navies of the world in perfect security. Often likened to San Francisco, it really has little in common with that great city, except, perhaps, that its business area and older suburbs are crowded about its waterfront, and cling to the steep slopes overlooking the harbour. The rest of the city spills over the hills to the harbour and sea-coast bays, or hides delightfully in the bush-filled valleys and hillsides of the hinterland.

Palmerston North (left)
Palmerston North spreads across the Rangitikei Plain some 129km (80 miles) north of Wellington — a cross-roads from which the main routes run out to Taranaki, Hawkes Bay and Auckland. The centre of the city is built around a gorgeously gardened square, through which the railway used to run before it was happily banished to the northern outskirts of the city. Billiard-table flat, the city exhibits, in spring, a glorious flowering of cherry trees.

63

Central Wellington. (left)
The fashion for the high-rise building began to flower in Wellington earlier than anywhere else in New Zealand. Chronically short of land, the early builders had to reclaim space from the harbour itself, and crowd many official buildings hard back against the harbourside cliffs. The winding, narrow street second from the left of the motorway, (centre), which almost exactly traces the original waterfront is still called Lambton Quay. But as commercial and Government enterprises grow, even the reclaimed land cannot easily accommodate them, so Wellington's centre now leaps upward in towers of steel and glass and concrete.

Wellington from Mount Victoria. (above)
Oriental Bay curves away from the foot of the hill, its modern apartment buildings still crowded cheek-by-jowl with narrow, tall old houses; and a curve of sandy beach stretches beyond the sea wall — a quite artificial creation, spread there by men, to give Wellingtonians a place to enjoy a dip and a sunbathe in weekends and lunch hours, when the city stifles in the summer heat.

Tugs, Mount Maunganui. (above left)
Mount Maunganui serves as Tauranga's deep-sea port. The port, which is situated on a narrow neck of the headland forming the eastern head of Tauranga Harbour, takes its name from Mount Maunganui proper, a 232m (762ft) eminence at the end of the headland. The port serves a huge paper pulp and forestry enterprise inland from the Bay of Plenty. On the ocean coast, Mount Maunganui Beach is famous and favoured for its splendid surf.

Tauranga Boat Harbour. (below left)
Tauranga Harbour, protected from the Pacific storms by the long, low Matakana Island, is highly favoured by small-boat enthusiasts. Deeply indented, with many small inlets of almost tropical appearance with their tall tree ferns leaning over the water like palm trees, and areas of mangrove, the harbour offers some 24km (15 miles) of superb boating water.

Lake Rotoroa, Hamilton. (right)
Rotoroa means, simply, "Long Lake." It lies beyond Hamilton's busy downtown centre, a peaceful place with gardened shores and shady trees and a population of magnificent black swans. Houses stand back from its shores, surrounded by colourful gardens. Huge Monarch butterflies are common here, and native birds — and the businesslike official towers of the city are just far enough beyond it all to heighten the feeling of tranquility.

Wairairapa Landscape. (left)
Much of the Wairarapa, when Europeans first came to it, was under heavy forest — in particular, an area known as Seventy Mile Bush. Hardy Scandinavian pioneers, on arrival in the district in which they had been allotted land, had first to become lumberjacks, felling the tall timber trees, clearing the forest, building their small communities wherever they managed to clear space to accommodate them. Then, as the timber was cut out, they returned to their original purpose and became farmers, establishing in these fertile valleys and on these rugged hills the farms which, today, are some of the most highly productive in the land.

Trelawney Stud, Near Cambridge. (above)
In the Waikato, on the rolling, gentle hills, racehorses are bred. The soft climate gives them year-round, free-range grazing, one of the secrets of their remarkable stamina; and on the training tracks in this lovely countryside, many a racecourse legend has had its beginnings. Yet the first association between this country and the horse had little to do with racing. Its first horses were almost certainly troopers' mounts, for this peaceful, rather English-looking countryside was once a wild military frontier between the Waikato and the King Country.

The Waiau Valley, near Wairoa, Hawkes Bay. (over page)
For all its quiet, its pastoral peace, its willows and poplars and orderly fields, the Waiau Valley is almost at the extreme edge of European man's conquest of the land. Just a little farther on, the Urewera Highlands rise up, wild and forested and unforgiving, still the homeland of the Tuhoe people, hardiest and most clannish, yet, as highlanders always seem to be, most hospitable of Maoris.

69

THE NORTH ISLAND COAST

There is, at the very northern tip of the North Island, a most dramatic meeting of the Pacific Ocean and the Tasman Sea. Eastwards and westward, they seem to have their own shades of blue and turquoise green, colours which change so subtly as the eye moves toward the meeting place of their waters that it would be impossible to tell where the one ceases and the other begins, were it not for the foam and fury, the eddy and chop where their currents clash.

From that point on, down the western and eastern coasts of the North Island, there is a general similarity. The west coast begins with the long, smooth sweep of Ninety Mile Beach, but soon breaks into a series of inlets and harbours — the Hokianga, which winds its way past huge sand dunes and penetrates a hilly landscape of farms and forest; the Kaipara, huge and many-branched, its inlets dotted with hamlet and township which, before adequate roads were pushed through, were served by a passenger ferry and cargo scows; the Manukau, shallow and broad; the Waikato rivermouth, Raglan and Kawhia. And then begins a series of beaches which run in sweeping curves to the rock-bound shores of West Cape and the North Taranaki Bight. High cliffs overhang black ironsand, which gives gradually to the golden sands of the South Taranaki Bight shores, in a single, sweeping curve southwards to Raumati and Paraparaumu and Waikanae; and then the coastline becomes reef-bound as it runs past Paekakariki, and the long Tasman swell, rolling in between the islands of Mana and Kapiti, crashes over the jagged rocks to the very base of the high bluffs. The road creeps past along a rocky ledge barely above the sea, presently to swing inland, over the hills to Wellington. But the shoreline swings around cliff and headland, past the shallow harbour of Porirua and the long inlet that runs into Pauatahanui; and it runs down, beneath the lofty hills of Makara and around Cape Terawhiti, along the Cook Strait shore to the magnificent harbour of Port Nicholson, Wellington.

The east coast, immediately south of North Cape, is broken and deeply indented with mangrove-fringed harbours — Parengarenga, Rangaunu Bay, and the perfect horseshoe shape of Doubtless Bay. Past that again, there is Whangaroa Harbour, long and zig-zagging, and then the fascinating Bay of Islands. Farther south, the shore is notched by Whangaruru Harbour, the double inlet of Parua Bay, the almost completely landlocked, splendidly sheltered Whangarei Harbour, and southward past the magnificent sweep of Bream Bay and the ragged Waiwera coastline to the broad, island-dotted

Piha, Auckland.
West coast beaches, by and large, seem wilder than those on the east coast. Piha, west of Auckland, is a favoured holiday resort which possesses a wild grandeur that makes holiday baches, bright swimsuits and the dark heads that bob in the mighty surf all but unnoticeable. Lion Rock, (so named because it resembles a couchant lion), the Piha Stream sweeping grandly into the sea by the lion's tail, and the bush-clad headlands combine in a spectacular seascape on which man has managed to make very little impression.

Whanarua Bay, Bay of Plenty. (above)
Where the Bay of Plenty coastline trends
north-eastward towards East Cape, it takes
a sudden turn due east between Waikawa
Point and Otiki Point, 12 or 13km (7 or 8
miles) of northward-facing small bays,
tree-fringed, reef-bound and encompassing
many delightfully sheltered little coves
such as Whanarua Bay, highly favoured
for holiday-making.

Kawa Kawa Bay, East Cape. (right)
North of East Cape, and immediately
south of Hicks Bay, Kawa Kawa Bay is
typical of the East Cape coves, with its
sandy beach and its wave-carved reefs,
lying isolated and lonely beneath
frowning, bush-clad cliffs. Here, in
December, the pohutukawa blazes scarlet
along the coastline, and the Pacific Ocean
pounds in towards the steep, high land.
Crayfish are caught here, the enormous
Packhorse variety.

Hauraki Gulf and Auckland's Waitemata Harbour. Eastwards from the
Gulf, across the Coromandel Peninsula, the Bay of Plenty presents some
320km (200 miles) of coastline, much of it in long curves of golden sand,
broken by the southward curving inlet of Mercury Bay, a number of smaller,
narrower inlets, Tauranga Harbour and Ohiwa Harbour, before curving
north-eastward to Cape Runaway. South of East Cape, the Pacific Ocean
beats into a long succession of small, sandy, reef-girt beaches, gouges out a
deep curve at Poverty Bay and takes a 160km (100 mile) bite into the land at
Hawke Bay. From Cape Kidnappers, it runs southward along sandy, reef-
protected beaches and open stretches of mighty surf, with the high, steep
hills uplifting almost from the water's edge, until it turns westward around
Cape Palliser and Black Rock, and the wide scoop of Palliser Bay, rounds
Cape Turakirae and Pencarrow Head, and enters Port Nicholson.

So both coasts possess an abundance of inlets and harbours, making them
a small-boat skipper's paradise, though the weather and the boisterousness
of the sea along the western side of the island can be daunting. Both, but
particularly the east coast, show a remarkable variety of scenery, from the
sub-tropical, mangrove-bordered harbours of Northland to surf-pounded
gravel beaches and severe cliffs along the edge of Cook Strait. There are
beaches protected by bush-crowned headlands, from whose sands a seeping
of hot water issues, in which the old-time Maoris and modern tourists have
bathed luxuriously, scooping hollows in the wet sand at low tide. There are
bays dotted with islets, and as famous for crayfish as the South Island's
Kaikoura coast ever was. There are, perhaps, fewer beaches rendered unsafe
by tidal rip and in-shore current than is the case in the South Island —
probably because the North Island's coastline is so much more irregular,
with jutting headlands and major capes foiling the ocean currents, diverting
them as a granite cliff diverts the most powerful river.

Western Coast of Coromandel Peninsula from Kirita Hill. (left)
Kirita Hill is a 394m (1,293ft) eminence overlooking Manaia Harbour and Kirita Bay, and affording a superlative view of the Hauraki Gulf. The islands just offshore are Wekarua and Rangipukea. Wekarua means "Nest of the Woodhen," which suggests that the old-time Maoris found the region an idyllic place whose shores and offshore waters provided seafoods, and even the offshore islets were rich storehouses of edible bird life — a region where the living was easy.

Matauri Bay, Northland. (above right)
Sheltered by a lofty headland, Matauri Bay is a glorious 1½km (¾ mile) stretch of golden sand, a little to the south-east of Whangaroa Harbour, on Northland's east coast. Commercial fishing is carried on in the bay, and five or six kilometres offshore lie the famed Cavalli Islands, favoured big-game fishing ground. Matauri Bay serves as a base for big-game fishing launches.

Lonely Cove, Coromandel Peninsula. (below right)
Lonely Cove is a short, broad sweep of golden sand, backed by tall limestone cliffs and a pleasant, pohutukawa-shaded grassy strip, all separated from the grander and more frequented strand of Cooks Beach by a tree-crowned headland. Its northern end is dominated by a tall bluff on which stand the Captain James Cook Memorial, commemorating Cook's visit to the area. As the monument's inscription says: "In this bay was anchored 5 - 15 November, 1796, HMS Endeavour, Lieutenant James Cook, Commander. He observed the Transit of Mercury and named this Bay."
The bay is named, of course, Mercury Bay, on which Lonely Cove is a minor indentation.

Mercury Bay, Coromandel Peninsula. (over page)
Mercury Bay is almost triangular, and lined with lesser bays and inlets and glorious sweeps of sandy beach. Here, on 4th November, 1769, Cook wrote in his journal: "My reasons for putting in here were the hopes of discovering a good harbour and the disire I had of being in some convenient place to observe the transit of Mercury ... If we should be so fortunate as to obtain this Observation the Longtitude of this place and Country will thereby be very accurately determined."

Hokianga Harbour, Northland. (left)
The Hokianga Harbour winds and twists
deep inland, past Opononi and Omapere.
Reaching through long, narrow inlets
between scrub-patched hills, it is the scene
of some of the earliest European history
in New Zealand, and the vicinity in which
Baron de Thierry tried to set up an
independent kingdom. The harbour
mouth is guarded by great, tawny
sandhills, and its shores are dotted with
small, picturesque villages, such as
Rawene and Kohukohu. The harbour
itself is shallow.

Matai Bay, Northland. (above)
The northern head of Doubtless Bay is a
rectangular peninsula, the northern
extremity of which is Cape Karikari. At
the base of this cape, a horseshoe curve of
white beach backed by rolling,
timber-patched country provides a small-
boat anchorage which is almost
landlocked. It is an idyllic little retreat
with, in patches, cabbage trees, tree ferns
and nikau palms to give it a tropical look.

Taupo Bay and Whangaroa Harbour, Northland. (above)
The little, clean, dazzling stretch of sand that marks Taupo Bay is lined with cottages and homes which look out across the blue water to Stephensons Island. The beach terminates in the steep and rocky face of the range of hills separating it from Whangaroa Harbour splendidly landlocked, with an entrance guarded by fantastic rock walls. Whangaroa was once a loading port for kauri timber; and here, in 1890, the ship *Boyd* called, and was attacked and burned by the Maoris in revenge for the flogging of the son of a chief, who had served aboard the ship.

Tongaporutu, Taranaki. (right)
Where the Tongaporutu River flows out into the North Taranaki Bight, some 56km (35 miles) north of New Plymouth, great sandstone cliffs stand, gnawed at by the restless Tasman Sea, riddled by it with caverns; and just off the southern head, at the river's mouth, is a sort of Maori Gibraltar, a castle-like rock which was held against attack until 1821 by Ngati-Tama warriors. In that year, the remnant of defenders abandoned it. The Tongaporutu River is navigable by launch for a distance of some 16km (10 miles) from its mouth, and is famed for its glorious scenery.

Because of the character of the New Zealand coast, European New Zealanders became seafarers from the earliest days of settlement. Communication between the coast-hugging little pioneer settlements was easier by sea than by land, and coastal shipping carried the bulk of the country's early trade. Oddly, though, the Maoris, whose ancestors came to New Zealand by deliberate feats of magnificent seamanship, largely deserted the ocean once they became settled, confining their navigation to river and lake, taking to the sea only for off-shore fishing.

Naturally, the earliest settlements were built close to the sea. The whalers, of course, planted their rumbustious bases in sheltered bays and coves, and the people who came to New Zealand in organised settlement schemes built their homes close to the shores on which they landed. The largest cities and towns, therefore, are either on the coast or on rivers which are, or once were, navigable. No New Zealander lives far from the sea, and most become joyously familiar with the white Pacific surf or the moody Tasman early in life, and look with pity upon those less favoured peoples whose beaches are fenced and swept and overwhelmingly crowded. It is the ambition of a majority of New Zealanders to retire somewhere near the sea, because the coast offers interest and recreation for people long after they have ceased taking an active part in mountain pursuits and other vigorous pastimes; and anyway, from the coast it is usually possible to look inland and see, on the far horizon, a pride of rugged peaks, especially from the west coast beaches. And that, of course, is possessing at last the best of both worlds.

Cape Kidnappers, Hawkes Bay. (above)
The sharp-edged ridge which droops
down like a dragon's tail, to end in island
spikes of rock, marks the southern
extremity of Hawke Bay. (Oddly, the
province is Hawkes Bay, and the bay itself
is Hawke Bay.) Here, on its razor-backed
crest, two flat platforms, devoid of
vegetation, are gannet colonies. The
gannet is a relative of the pelican. He
rarely nests on mainland sites, usually
choosing small, steep-sided offshore
islands.

84

Captain Cook Statue, Gisborne. (left)
The visit of Captain Cook to Poverty Bay
was not a particularly happy one,
apparently, for he found the Maoris here
unwilling to trade fresh provisions, and
even reluctant to allow him to replenish
his fresh water supply — in complete
contrast to the inhabitants of the shores to
the north, whose open-handedness caused
him to name the region Bay of Plenty.
Behind this statue, which stands on
Gisborne's foreshore, is the distant
headland he called Young Nick's Head,
after a cabin boy, Nicholas Young, who
first sighted it.

Tongue Point, Wellington. (above)
Jutting out into Cook Strait, about 6½km
(4 miles) south-east of Cape Terawhiti,
and 12km (7½ miles) west of the entrance
to Wellington Harbour, Tongue Point,
with its narrow, shingly beach walled by
steep bluffs and high hills, and with its
isolated spread of green pasture, is
buffeted by the Cook Strait gales. From it,
slightly hazy with distance, may be seen
the Marlborough hills of the South
Island, rising up across a mere 40km (25
miles) of somewhat turbulent sea.

Urquhart Bay, Whangarei. (below)
Where the Pacific flows into Whangarei
Harbour, it swirls around Marsden Point,
gouging out a broad curve on the
opposite shore which is called Urquhart
Bay. Over the bay stands a 404m (1,325ft)
peak known as Manaia, named after a
chieftain of olden time who sent his
principal fighting chief off to battle
distant enemies, then stole his wife. The
outraged husband returned and attacked
Manaia's *pa*, and chased Manaia, his two
children and his faithless wife. Before he
could kill them, the gods turned them all
into stone, and there they can be seen to
this day, pillars of rock on top of the
bluff.

Anaura Bay, East Coast. (right)
The bush is gone, replaced by sheep and
cattle, and the *whares* on the hillsides
have been supplanted by small houses
here and there; but Captain Cook would
still recognise the cove he visited in 1769.
He came ashore with a watering party and
sat on the hillside above the bay to make a
slightly quaint little sketch of sailors
filling barrels, and Pourewa Island, which
he called Sporing Island, after the
assistant naturalist. He would find, today,
a small marker on a plateau overlooking
the lovely beach, relating how he got
wood and water, and Joseph Banks and
Daniel Solander collected plants, one
warm day in October, 1769.

*Kirita Bay, Coromandel Peninsula.
(above)*
Below Kirita Hill and opening into the
Hauraki Gulf, Kirita Bay looks out across
the Gulf, at the mouth of the Firth of
Thames, to the ancient volcanic humps
which rise up south of the Waitemata
Harbour and Auckland, 26km (16 miles)
across the calm Hauraki waters. The
whole of the peninusla's western coast is
notched with such calm and sheltered
coves.

Piercy Rock, Bay of Islands. (right)
The eastern headland of the entrance to
the Bay of Islands is a slim finger of land
called Cape Brett, and some little distance
offshore, looking like a piece of the cape
which has been broken off and tossed
carelessly into the water, stands Piercy
Island, better known to thousands of
tourists and fishermen as The Hole in the
Rock. The cavern which pierces the
sharp-topped pinnacle on this miniature
Gibraltar is lofty enough to allow
pleasure launches to sail through it.

Te Araroa (left)
Spread along the curve of a bay between
Hicks Bay and East Cape, Te Araroa lies
beneath a lofty, scarred bluff. With the sea
at its feet, and the sandy beaches and
occasional reefs along its shoreline, it is a
favourite holiday spot. Te Araroa
possesses an enormous, venerable
Pohutukawa tree, claimed to be the largest
in New Zealand, and possibly the oldest.

*East Cape and Pohutukawa Tree. (above
right)*
On this eastern most finger of land,
beyond which there is nothing but empty
ocean for thousands of miles, the hills are
eroded and gaunt, and the sea winds, salt-
laden, whipping along the beaches, bend
the gnarled, tough pohutukawa trees and
scorch the grasses. This country is sheep
country, the inhabitants still
predominantly Maori, enjoying a life-style
which still contains essential elements of
their ancient ways.

Pohutukawa Blossoms. (below right)
For all that it clings to rocky coastal cliffs
and wind-parched, battered shores, the
pohutukawa, gnarled and twisted,
sometimes even stunted, by the harsh
conditions of its environment, still
produces, year by year, a Christmas-tide
blaze of scarlet blooms, each apparently
delicate. There is a legend that when the
first Maoris arrived in New Zealand, they
saw pohutukawa blossoms along the
shores, and promptly threw away the
prized but faded red ceremonial feathers
they had brought from their tropical
homeland, and gathered the blossoms,
only to find that they faded and fell apart
very quickly.

Bay of Islands, from Rawhiti. (left)
Rawhiti is a scattered farming community
on the long, writhing tail of land that
terminates in Cape Brett. From its hilltops
a magnificent panoramic view of the Bay
of Islands spreads westward and
northward. Urupukapuka and several
smaller islands sprawl offshore, across the
Albert Channel, and in an inlet on the
island's southern side is the big-game
fishing base known as Zane Grey's Camp.

Russell, Bay of Islands. (above)
The peaceful and rather quaint little town
of Russell was once Kororareka, easy
winner of the title "Hell-Hole of the
Pacific." It was a base for whalers, sealers,
traders and all the sweepings of the seas.
Noisy with grog shops, it was eventually
burned to the ground by outraged Maoris
— all except the Anglican Christ Church,
which is still scarred with bullet holes,
and Bishop Pompallier's House. Both
buildings were respected as mission
property, and spared by the Maoris.

Wainui Bay, Northland. (left)
Between Whangaroa Harbour and
Matauri Bay, where the hills come down
to the Pacific, another of Northland's
delightful sweeps of clean yellow sand,
Wainui Bay, is one of New Zealand's
lesser known holiday resorts. With its
occasional rocky reefs, its gently shelving
shore, its grassy headlands and its
pohutukawa, it lies at the end of a
twisting, somewhat steep hill road from
Whangaroa.

Matai Bay, Northland. (above)
The small headland that juts into the blue
waters of Matai Bay is tipped with a
broken outcropping of rock, forming rock
pools which are alive with shellfish,
starfish and the myriad forms of tidal
marine life.

Gannet Colony, Cape Kidnappers. (left)
The gannets that nest on the dragon-tail promontory of Cape Kidnappers are the Australian gannet, large white birds with yellow heads and black wingtips. They feed on small fish, and nest in November through December. This gannet rookery is believed to be the only mainland rookery in the world. Usually the birds nest on small, rocky, offshore islands.

Karikari Bay, Northland. (above right)
On the northern side of that peninsula which encloses Doubtless Bay, Karikari Bay lies open to the Pacific Ocean. The country behind it is comparatively low-lying, with sand dunes and, dramatic in its shape and its sudden elevation, an ancient volcanic cone on the western end of the beach.

Castlepoint Lighthouse, Wairarapa Coast. (below right)
The fine, sandy, gently shelving beach at Castlepoint terminates dramatically in an upward-sloping reef, spreading below a rocky bluff whose limestone pinnacles give the place its name. A stretch of this reef encloses a small lagoon like a man-made sea wall, and at its northern end, the grassy-topped bastion thrusts out into deep water, lifting a slender spire of lighthouse at its tip, like an exclamation point, drawing attention to the fact that here, for coastal vessels, is danger.

Mount Maunganui Beach. (left)
From the foot of Maunganui, ancient
fortress-hill, the beach curves southward,
fronting the low-lying isthmus which
forms the southern "breakwater" of
Tauranga's harbour. Once the scene of
bloody battles, this beach is now one of
New Zealand's best-known and most
favoured holiday resorts, especially
popular with surfers.

*Yacht Harbour and Mount Victoria,
Wellington. (above)*
Tucked in between the Overseas Passenger
Terminal and the sandy stretch of beach
at Oriental Bay, the Wellington Yacht
Harbour is a still, calm haven on which
colourful pleasure craft bob gently at
moorings like waterlilies on a pond. The
hillside suburb of Roseneath climbs the
northern and western slopes of Mount
Victoria, the houses clustered about the
old convent like a medieval village
gathered about its castle.

Cape Reinga, Northland.
Cape Reinga is not quite the northernmost part of New Zealand, but is near enough to it to have become, in Maori lore, the departing place of the spirits of the dead. It juts out to form the eastern extremity of Spirits Bay, and the Tasman Sea and the Pacific Ocean meet at its tip in a fine fury of conflicting currents.

Makarori Beach is one of several East Cape seaside resorts just north of Gisborne. The warm climate and open sandy beaches sometimes shaded by huge Pohutukawa trees ensure that Makarori, Wainui and similar adjacent resorts are well populated during summer months.

THE BEAUTY OF NEW ZEALAND'S
SOUTH ISLAND

THE SOUTHERN ALPS.

A first-time visitor to New Zealand, describing his impressions, might well say, simply, "The country is mountainous." It wouldn't be telling the full tale, but such a description would convey a fairly adequate picture. New Zealand *is* mountainous; and even in those areas where it is not, its plains, coastlines, lakes, cities, rolling pastoral landscapes are brooded over, dominated by mountains. Wherever the eye looks inland, it is guided on and upwards to a high, serrated skyline, sometimes dark with forest to the crests of its notched ridges, sometimes dazzling with year-round snow. Single summits, or prides of powerful peaks, mountains are the predominant feature, the landscape rampant, the key component which establishes the character of the entire scene.

This, in varying degrees, is true of both North and South Islands. But it is in the South Island that the mountains reach a perfection of grandeur. The South Island is more spectacularly creased than the North Island. Viewed from almost any internal airline flight, vast areas of it are seen to be as crumpled as a discarded piece of paper, with range upon range of titanic pressure-fold ridges, dovetailed or massively tangled chains of peaks, stretching away for as far as the eye can see.

The Tasman Mountains, the Richmond Range, the St. Arnaud and Spenser Mountains and the Kaikoura Ranges fan out northward from the great rugged chain and uprising forested spurs which rise up to form the Southern Alps; and the Southern Alps, at their southern end, fray out into a wild and well-nigh impenetrable tangle and knotting of mountains covering perhaps half of the Otago-Southland region.

The Southern Alps, of course, take pride of place. They are the show-piece, the magnificent spectacle, that attracts visitors in their awed thousands. In their folds and in the pleatings of their skirts they hold lakes of unrivalled splendour. On their valley-riven flanks, between their massive lateral arms, they cradle splendid glaciers. In this massif alone there are more than a hundred and thirty peaks that rise over 2,400 metres, chief of which is *Aorangi,* the Cloud Piercer, officially and prosaically named Mount Cook by official and prosaic Captain Stokes of H.M.S. *Acheron,* after the great 18th century navigator.

It is the mountains, of course, that order the country's climate. The South Island is exactly what its name describes, a southern ocean island, with an island's capricious weather patterns. That is to be expected. What is astonishing, however, is the number of climatic variations, distinct climatic zones, within such a small compass; for the island is a mere 750km long by 250km wide at its widest point. And that — by continental terms — is a small area in which to have, side-by-side, zones which are temperate in climate, with a moderate to low rainfall, areas which are dry to the point of being

Snowfall, Craigieburn Range, Canterbury.

The Cragieburn Range, high above Lake Lyndon on the road to Arthurs Pass, is a drab area in summer, more like a gigantic gravel heap than an alpine spur. But in winter, when the snow is down into the valleys, it is at once majestic and magical, like everyone's dream of Switzerland, or a memory of European Christmases.

Lake Tekapo, Mackenzie Country. (above)
A true alpine lake, Lake Tekapo was once an ancient glacier, a prehistoric ice-burden which the surrounding countryside has never quite forgotten or forgiven. Near the lake's verge, the feathery snowgrass, foxglove and the spiny matagouri seem to be all that is willing to inhabit the thin soil covering the ancient moraine.

Glendhu Bay, Lake Wanaka. (right)
Though the autumn days are warm, the shingly beach of Glendhu Bay is deserted by evening, when the last rays of the lowering sun are defeated by the early evening chill, and the cold comes creeping across the deep waters of Lake Wanaka which, it is suddenly easy to recall, was once a mass of glacier ice, thousands of metres thick.

near-desert, areas of immoderately high rainfall and lush forest of almost sub-tropical luxuriance, areas which experience each winter a heavy and sustained snowfall, areas of crackling frosts, and areas with an enviable tally of annual sunshine hours.

The moisture-laden winds from the Tasman Sea bring clouds which are literally trapped on the western side of the Southern Alps, and are forced to such altitudes that they precipitate heavily on the narrow coastal strip on the mountains' western side. The north-west winds, buffeting their way through mountain valleys as through gigantic wind-tunnels, burst upon the eastern plains with great and sometimes destructive force.

The eternal snows upon those prodigious peaks refrigerate the winter air, so that east-coast towns, cities and farmlands receive a disinfecting poultice of frost on clear nights from late March till late September.

No South Islander lives more than two or three hours' drive from ski-slopes, ice-bound skating ponds and lakes and snowy hillsides from July to October. Few have not at least a nodding acquaintance with the high country, and some memorable experiences of the great ranges, or at least of some memorable mountain mood or spectacle, such as the first rays of the morning sun touching Mount Cook's summit with flame while the land is still dark with night, or the last pink glow of the setting sun, or the reflected mirror-brightness of the moonlight on the snow-clad face of the Remarkables, or the snow-covered peaks of the Kaikouras seeming to lean over the calm bay. No matter where South Islanders live — on the broad, billiard-table-flat plains of Canterbury, or the rolling hills of North Otago, or the rock-bound Kaikoura coast, or in the high upland basins of Amuri or the Mackenzie Country, or the rock-ribbed, glacier-planed terraces of Central Otago, or in the bustling towns and cities — every South Islander is, in some special way, a child of the mountains.

Mount Talbot, Fiordland. (above left)

As you drive across Lyttles Flat, where the Homer Tunnel construction village once stood, and which is now hutless, and fragrant with fern and mountain gentian, Mount Talbot, 2,225m (7,300ft), stands before you, its twisted peak retaining pockets of snow all year round. Part of the Barrier Range, a spur of the Darran Mountain complex, the forbidding peak leans back from huge fans of avalanche rock.

Ailsa Mountains, Hollyford Valley, Fiordland. (below left)

From where the Milford Road runs through the Hollyford Valley, the Ailsa Mountains, (right), trend away south-eastward, walling off that jungle-like, beautiful wilderness from the Upper Greenstone Valley. Some of the finest tramping trails in the world wander through these primeval fastnesses.

Glendhu Bay, Lake Wanaka: (right)

A pleasant curve of beach, lined with willow and pine and adding a touch of gentleness to the bulbous, rocky faces of Glendhu Bluff and the stern mountain surroundings, Glendhu Bay is popular with swimmers, in the burning summer heat. In autumn it becomes a favourite haunt of anglers, fishing for brown and rainbow trout and Atlantic salmon.

Lake Ianthe, Westland. (below)

Set in a scenic reserve about 15km from Harihari, this delightful little gem of a lake was named, it is said, by a surveyor-explorer who admired Byron's "Childe Harold's Pilgrimage," which was dedicated to a little girl named Ianthe. If that seems to be a roundabout way of arriving at a name, perhaps the little (5.6 square kilometres) water's very smallness, and the fact that exquisite beauty in so compact a package, by its very contrast with the grandeur of the mountains, brought to mind simple and intimate and charming things.

Bowen Falls, Milford Sound. (above)

Bowen Falls issue from a hanging valley high above the head of Milford Sound. The water plunges, first, onto an inclined, hollowed rock "springboard," from which it leaps out again in a sparkling white arc, to fall into a spray-clouded basin. The leap is most dramatic after rain; but even when the water is draped over the rocky faces of the gash in the forested mountain wall, it is hardly less beautiful.

Clinton Canyon, Milford Track. (far left)

Part of the famous Milford Track winds beside the Clinton River for 23km (14 miles) through the mountain-walled valley known as the Clinton Canyon. The forested mountains rise straight up from the valley floor for perhaps 1,200m (4,000ft), then lean back as they stab skyward with spear-point peaks to some 1,830m (6,000ft) above sea level. The canyon climbs, eventually, to Mackinnon Pass, reaching up through moss-hung, twisted mountain beeches to an open area of ranunculus and mountain daisy, where *keas* come close, unafraid and friendly.

Fox Glacier. (left)

Fox Glacier's somewhat zig-zagging course brings the great ice-river down from the neve, the vast, eternal snowfields in their inclined basin between the Fritz and Fox Ranges, to a landscape of spurs covered with forest of almost tropical luxuriance.From the glacier's terminal face issues the Fox River, bursting out from an ice cave,carrying great chunks of ice as it hurries down to join the Cook River.

The Okuru River and South Westland Mountains. (above)

From Okuru, south of Haast, the great forested humps of hill stand up above bush and swamp to form outriders of Mount Aspiring National Park, southern extremity of the Alps proper. This is untouched country — the snow-fed river, swelled by many a tributary creek, sliding across the coastal flats, flanked by sedges and flax, with a backing of shrubs, which in turn give way to tall forest trees.

*High Country Road near Glenmore
Station, Mackenzie Country. (above)*

Towards the head of Lake Tekapo, in the
brown snowgrass-and-tussock landscape of
the Mackenzie Country with its shelter
belts of dark, hardy pine, the Godley
Peaks rise up, snow-covered in winter, but
in summer eroded and barren, like
gigantic heaps of gravel, crumbling slowly
to choke the Canterbury rivers and build
up the vast gravel flats of the Mackenzie
Basin.

*Shotover River at Arthurs Point, Central
Otago. (right)*

All the fascinating contradictions of the
Central Otago landscape, (right), show in
the Shotover River's writhing valley, near
Queenstown. Here are the typical rock-
ribbed hills, furred with brown, sun-
scorched grasses and patched with
matagouri and tough briars. Here are the
poplars and willows, autumn-yellow as
the first frosts paint them; and amidst the
harshness there is, here and there, the lush
green of a cultivated field. But always,
winding across the scene, are the Central
Otago rivers, depositing their frequently
gold-bearing gravels at the feet of rocky,
broom-cladspurs.

Lake Te Anau. (above)

Biggest of the South Island's lakes is Te Anau, its western shores towered over by the densely forested Murchison Mountains, its eastern side gentle with willow and bluegum where an easy, rolling countryside comes down to its shore. In the dark mountains, in 1948, two fascinating discoveries were made. By a small tarn, high in the mountains, tracks led to the finding of a bird long thought to be extinct, the colourful *takahe;* and near the lake's shore, almost directly beneath the tarn, the legendary and long forgotten Te Ana-Au Caves were uncovered, with their glow-worm displays rivalling those of Waitomo.

Lake Quill and Sutherland Falls. (right)

Cupped in the mountains of the Milford Sound district, Lake Quill pours a steady stream of water from a jug-like lip, to form Sutherland Falls, highest in New Zealand and third highest in the world. The first leap of the falls is a lofty 288m (815ft), the second 229m (751ft) and the third 103m (338ft). The Sutherland Falls are one of the principal attractions along the world-famed Milford Track. When Lake Quill is in flood, the Sutherland Falls curve out in a single, spectacular leap of 1,904ft.

Lakes Tekapo and Alexandrina, from Mount John: (above)

The Mackenzie Country lakes are of two kinds — snow-fed and rain-fed. Snow-fed lakes, like Tekapo, are a beautiful lapis-lazuli blue, and rain-water lakes, like Alexandrina, are green-glass clear. The Mackenzie Basin, a region named after the Scottish Highland shepherd who discovered it, (and tried to stock it with stolen sheep), is a wild expanse of tussock and snowgrass and clear mountain air. On Mount John has been set an observatory, to take advantage of the clear, dry atmosphere.

117

Mount Tasman, from Fox, South Westland (below)

The peaks of the Southern Alps are never more spectacular, never more clearly, magnificently displayed, than they are from South Westland, that narrow coastal shelf at their very feet. Mount Tasman, 3,498m (11,475ft), cradles on its faces the snows which feed the Balfour and Abel Janzoon Glaciers, the latter spilling down into the vast neve which give birth to the mighty Fox Glacier.

Fox Glacier from Clearwater Flat. (left)

The Clearwater River rattles over stony shallows along the edge of a typical Westland river flat, which it shares with the Cook River. Its waters reflect the almost theatrical spectacle of clouds slowly parting like stage curtains to reveal, first the Fox Glacier in its notch in the granite mountains, and then the splendour of the stupendous peaks from which it flows.

Mount Cook and Sealy Tarn.

Mount Cook, Aorangi, the Cloud-Piercer,
New Zealand's highest mountain, with the
long chain of peaks trailing southward to
form an impressive wall on the eastern
side of the Hooker Glacier, is awe-
inspiring country. From Sealy Tarn, little
can be seen of the Hooker Glacier but the
long heaping of gravel and boulders
which it has left behind in its retreat back
into the high reaches beneath Turner Peak
and Proud Pass. But in mountain
meadows such as this grow the famed
Mount Cook lily, *(Ranunculus Lyellii,
upper right),* and the mountain daisy,
(Celmisia), lower right, which, in season,
are a sight worth seeing.

Lake Matheson, Westland. (over)

Lake Matheson, near Fox Glacier in South
Westland, is a more familiar sight to most
New Zealanders and many overseas visitors
than far bigger lakes — because the
quality of its mountain reflections makes
this bush-fringed little water a favourite
photographic subject. It was once a huge
block of ice, left behind in ancient times
by the receding glacier, and the forest
which crowds down to its brim grows over
a moraine which was left behind, marking
a stage in the glacier's early growth, before
it began its long retreat.

Westland Bush and Stream (left)
On the western side of the ranges, where the rainfall is frequent and heavy, the bush has an almost tropical luxuriance. Living trees are coated, furred, festooned with parasitic growth. Dead forest giants lie on the forest floor, crumbling beneath a burden of fungi and mosses. An unbelievable variety of ferns peers from flying-buttress root systems of trees, or reach for the sky on rough, palm-like trunks. Strange and riotous growth clothes mossy banks and droops from host trees; and the whole struggling growth fights upward, competing for a share of sunshine.

Lake Brunner from Lone Tree Lookout, Westland. (below)
When they found it in its high setting of forested foothills, Europeans named it Lake Brunner. The Maori, perhaps more alive to the poetry of its calm beauty, had long before named it *Moana Kotuku,* the Sea of the White Heron. Whatever it is called, this beautiful water is just that, a vista of calm loveliness spreading across 26 square kilometres, (16 square miles), largest of all the Westland lakes. It is constantly replenished by the runoff of Westland's heavy and frequent rains in the surrounding mountains.

Sheep Mustering Beneath Mount Cook, Mackenzie Country. (over above)
In the Canterbury high country, merino sheep graze all through summer on the sparse, sun-ripened grasses, foraging over the tops of hills which, in another country would be listed among the high mountains. But always, snow-covered Mount Cook and the central massif of the Southern Alps gaze down upon the dun-coloured pastures, and chill with their snows the breath of the westerly winds, even in high summer.

Mount Aspiring, Southern Alps. (far right)

The great spire of Mount Aspiring soars 3,135m (9,957ft), into the sky, towering above the surrounding peaks of Stargazer, Mt Joffre, Mt French, Moonraker, MtAvalanche — a great white fang of a peak after which is named the Mount Aspiring National Park, a wilderness of eternally snow-covered tops and deep, densely forested valleys spreading over an immense 287,205ha.

Ski-Plane on Tasman Glacier. (right)

The Tasman Glacier, sweeping down like a gleaming 29km (18-mile) staircase from beneath the 3,109m (10,200ft) peak of Mt Elie de Beaumont to the gravelly valley of the Tasman River, may be climbed. But it is more easily, more spectacularly mounted in a ski-plane, which flies its passengers around the mighty peaks, and lands you on the glacier's neve, a matchlessly thrilling experience.

The Lighthouse, Skippers Road, Queenstown. (above)

The famous — or infamous — road that wanders and climbs precariously through Skippers Canyon leads into a harsh landscape, where the rocky frame of the mountains bursts out through the thin, parched soil, and rock, formations have inspired fanciful names, like the Lighthouse, (above.) Perhaps the gold-fossickers found it comforting, in this unforgiving land, to imagine that such features might have been raised by men's hands rather than rudely sculpted, as they were, by climatic severity.

Remarkables Landscape, near Queenstown. (above right)

As if relenting briefly, Central Otago now and again smiles in scenes of pastoral peace, (right, above), such as these green and pleasant fields at the foot of the stern Remarkables Range — pockets of sun-trapped fertility amid the rugged mountains. The Remarkables, with peaks over 2,100m (7,000ft) high, and harsh, seamed faces, loom over Lake Wakatipu and make the soft pastures seem even more gentle by comparison. But even in these grassy fields, the hardy Merino and Corriedale do best, thriving where other breeds would succumb to the fierce alpine climate.

Lake Alexandrina, Mackenzie Country. (below right)

Lake Alexandrina, (right), close to Lake Tekapo, forms a soft and comfortable oasis in the quilted landscape of brown hills. Even the water looks different from that of its neighbour, for this lake is rain-fed, not snow-fed. From the air, the contrasting colours of the snow-fed and rain-fed lakes of the Mackenzie Basin give an impression of jewels in a golden setting.

Skippers Bridge and the Upper Shotover River. (above)

Into the dark and forbidding mountain country, in the 1860s, came thousands of gold-seekers; and the Shotover River, (above), rewarded many of them richly. From others it witheld its wealth, and yet others it drowned, trapping them in its sudden floods, in deep and rocky gorges. In this kind of country man's engineering appears frail and spidery beside the superlative landscape of rock and crag.

Frankton Arm, Lake Wakatipu, and the Remarkables. (left)

The Frankton Arm of Lake Wakatipu pokes eastward from the main body of the lake, running beneath the rugged faces of the Remarkables Range, lapping the geometrically square shore of the peninsula at Queenstown, and the pine-covered tip of Kelvin Heights peninsula. The township of Frankton spreads itself down to the water's edge, where the lake waters gather for a turbulent rush through the Kawarau Gorge.

131

Tasman Glacier Skifield, Southern Alps. (above)

The Tasman Glacier skifield is not, as one might think, a fast, downhill 29km run, but rather something of a ski-travelling journey over slopes of varying steepness, traversing flats and mounds, for a distance of about 8km. It is principally a wonderful wander amongst magnificent alpine scenery — but the guides recommend it only for experienced skiers.

Hooker Glacier, Southern Alps. (right)

The Empress, Noeline and Mona Glacier, pushing down from Endeavour Col on the Mount Cook Range, are brought up short by the high wall of rock where the Baker Saddle climbs between La Perouse and the lesser Dilemma Peak. Not to be denied, they swing southward, combining into one great ice-fall, the Hooker Glacier, comparatively short, steep and spectacular.

Tui Tarn, Cass River, Mackenzie Country.
(left)

There are two Cass Rivers in Canterbury
— but to trampers of the bare, almost sub-
antarctic upland of the Mackenzie, the
best-known Cass River is the one which
runs down from a high valley between the
Liebig and Hall Ranges to Lake Tekapo.
Though its domain is bare and
windswept, it possesses the lonely, wild
glory reflected in the still, cold waters of
Tui Tarn.

*Lake Ohau, Mackenzie Country. (below
right)*

Like other lakes of glacial origin, Ohau is
surrounded by superb mountain scenery,
the high, snow-covered ranges rising from
the water's edge; and close to the tourist
lodge, which sits on this broad shelf
overlooking the lake, is a fine skifield.
Ohau is the southernmost of the
Mackenzie Country lakes, and perhaps the
most spectacular, being more like the
alpine lakes of Central Otago than are
Tekapo, Pukaki or Alexandrina. At an
altitude of 524m (1,720ft), Ohau spreads
over 23 square miles.

Lindis Pass Hills. (right)

The Lindis Pass, where a narrow, dusty
road slips through from the Mackenzie
Basin to Central Otago, is a place of snow
and floods in winter, and of oven-like heat
in summer, when the hills are baked,
brown and resemble the folds of a
carelessly dropped blanket. The Lindis
Pass was known to the old-time Maoris,
who wandered frequently over its 1,006m
(3,300ft) altitude.

*Purakaunui Falls, South Otago. (over
page)*

Purakaunui Falls, in the Catlins District
of South Otago, is an exquisitely set
cascade in a tract of native forest, on
steeply falling land near the coast. Easily
reached by a walkway from the road, the
falls are rapidly becoming a premier
tourist attraction. (Though the setting is
beautiful, the name has unpleasant
associations. It means "Big Stack of
Firewood," and is a contemptuous
reference to the bodies of Maori warriors
slain in one of their olden tribal battles,
and stacked ready for cooking and eating.)

Lake Hawea, Otago.

Lake Hawea, lying in the bed of a
prehistoric glacier, is some 48 square miles
in area — 35km (22 miles) long, and up to
8km (5 miles) wide. Magnificently
overlooked by the range which runs
between Mount Grandview and Dingle
Peak, the lake has that frequently found
quality of mirror stillness which seems to
be characteristic of lakes of glacial origin;
and when the dusk gathers early, as it does
in such deep mountain valleys, the high,
still-daylit clouds are reflected perfectly in
the glassy water, giving back a second-
hand light which holds back the darkness
on the valley floor for a little while
longer.

Tree Fern Fronds.

In the Westland rain forests, at the feet of
the high Alps, on that narrow shelf
between the mountains and the sea, the
tree ferns, (right), grow to prodigious size,
their budding, violin-neck fronds opening
out, palm-tree-like, to sway and wave
along the roadsides at the edge of the dark
bush. Such fronds were a frequent element
in the art of the Maori carver.

Buller River at Lake Rotoroa, Nelson Lakes District. (top left)

Where the main alpine chain frays out at its northern end into a fantastic tangle of complicated ranges, in a region criss-crossed with deep rift valleys, lie Lakes Rotoiti and Rotoroa, set like jewels in the forested mountains; and from Lake Rotoroa, the larger of the two, issues the Buller River, lusty and powerful and deep, right from its source and all the way down to the Tasman Sea.

Upper Waimakariri, Canterbury. (above)

The upper reaches of the Waimakariri (Cold Waters) River, where it wanders out from the high alps, are a tangled skein of gravel-choked waterways, subject to sudden floods, (which, in a more populous area, would be massively destructive), when the snows melt or there are heavy rains in the mountain valleys. The Waimakariri, like the Rangitata and the Rakaia, waters the broad Canterbury Plain, which, indeed, these mountain-bred rivers helped to form, by bringing gravels down from the mountainsides and depositing them in the shallow sea which once washed the skirts of the foothills.

Upper Wairau River, Marlborough. (below left)

The Wairau River begins in a long fold in that crumpled country east of the Spenser Mountains. It tumbles down through high-altitude beech forests into a fen and tussock basin beneath Mount Alma, and swings sharply northward, to brawl and foam beneath the eastern faces of the St Arnaud Range, in a forest-filled valley, as it flows on its way to the Pacific Ocean.

Lake Marian and Mount Crosscut. (left)
Tucked into the folds of the mountains, at the head of the Marian Valley in the Hollyford region of Fiordland, Lake Marian lies below the Lyttle Falls, which leap down from a hanging valley holding two more small lakes. In this valley, which runs east-west between the precipitous and imposing faces of Mount Christine and Mount Crosscut — in this almost overpowering area — a Surveyor-General, E.H.Wilmot, chose to bestow the name of a young cousin. Not only did he name the valley after her, but also the sublime little lake, plus two lakes near the head of the falls, which he named Mariana and Marianette, a dainty nomenclature for such a powerful landscape.

Craigieburn Skifield. (above)
On the road that leads from Christchurch to Arthurs Pass, there are some four fine skifields, mostly operated by ski clubs — family fields, a mere hour and a half by car from Christchurch. The Craigieburn field has a rope tow and other essential facilities; nothing large or opulent, but enough to ensure skiers of all levels of skills, competitive skiers, fun skiers and complete tyros, a good day's fun for a good price. On the slopes in this area, the Forestry Department has been conducting a trial planting of pines, which will serve to hold together slopes which, when not under snow, erode massively.

MAN'S HAND — THE SOUTH ISLAND

Even surrounded by a superabundance of natural beauty, man still has other needs. He might not live by bread alone, but bread he must have to live at all. So he drills and marshalls his landscape until it functions like his own machinery, to feed and clothe and house him. Also, though there are a few exceptional people for whom the untamed wilderness is all they need, there are many more for whom the wild beauty is better taken in small sips. The mass of people, though they enjoy the grandeur of mountains and the riotous growth of the bush, have a need for ordered paths, barbered lawns and disciplined, flowery gardens.

In addition, those brave souls who first abondoned their familiar English scene to settle in a new and alien land experienced a crushing homesickness. To aleviate its very real pain, they hastened to establish in their new soil the style of buildings, even the trees, flowers, animals and birds they had known and loved in the Old Country.

Yet it could never be a real duplication. For one thing, there was so much more land to spare. Farms were measured in thousands of acres, sheep runs in hundreds of square miles, rather than the neat, small, intensely cultivated holdings of rural England, measured in fifties or hundreds of acres. Every householder was encouraged to build his home on a half-acre or quarter-acre section, with the result that populations which would have fitted easily into a small cluster of semi-detached cottages bordering a quarter of a mile of English road, here sprawled over a square mile of perfectly farmable landscape; and the larger centres sprawled outward over areas that would have contained an English city.

Even architecture could not entirely reproduce the familiar English scene. The traditional methods of building were not entirely suitable. Nogging, for example, that style of building which is usually labelled "Tudor," though it is much older than that, consisting of an exposed framing with the bricks laid in between the frame members, proved unsatisfactory in New Zealand because of the ferocious shrinkage coefficient of New Zealand timbers. The ancient stone houses and ecclesiastical buildings which, in England, had stood for centuries had not had to cope with the not infrequent earthquakes in this geologically younger land.

So architecture and building practices became a sort of compromise, out of which has grown some original and striking innovations.

Some native trees did provide some exceptionally fine building timbers; but the best of such timbers were slow-growing; and, moreover, early

Lily Gigantum, Mount Peel Homestead Grounds, Canterbury.

Old World trees and Old World wildflowers create an English woodland of stately oak and trumpets of Lily Gigantum in country which must have seemed, to the first Mount Peel settlers, to be a dreary, alien, tussock-covered wilderness at the feet of the overbearing mountains.

The Christchurch Town Hall and Ferrier Fountain. (above)

On the banks of the principal stream, the Pilgrims' descendents built their Town Hall complex, purely New Zealand in its architecture, yet somehow as English as a medieval castle. And in its courtyard, to offset its severity, they set fountains like giant thistledown.

Daffodils, Botanical Gardens, Christchurch. (right)

On a swampy site, in heavy soil laced with a network of peaty streams, the Canterbury Pilgrims built a city. In its midst, they reserved 497 acres of hard-won ground, to serve as a park and a garden, so that city dwellers would never lack for out-door spaces; and in the middle of the park, they planted a garden of English trees, and patched the greensward with beds of daffodils, so that spring in the heart of Christchurch would always remind them of April in England . . .

146

Christchurch Cathedral, and Cathedral Square. (above)

At the city's heart, they raised a Gothic cathedral, to denote the nature of their settlement and the direction of their own ideals. For the Canterbury Pilgrims were principally a Church of England band, and the Church originally undertook their pastoral and educational care. It was planned from the first that Christchurch should have a public school, (English style), and a University; and the University Chapel was to double as a Cathedral. Circumstances changed these schemes somewhat, but the Cathedral was built where originally the school and university were to have stood — in the centre of the city.

exploitation brought at least one species to the verge of extinction. Certain exotic trees, notably the radiata pine, were found to grow rapidly and well — so over the past fifty years, vast areas have been planted, hundreds of square miles of geometrically rectangular stands, tidily, rigidly separated into dark green regiments by access road and fire-break.

The rivers which flow mightily down to the ocean from upland lake and permanent snowfield have proved to be eminently harnessable for the production of electric power, or the irrigation of otherwise waste areas, or both. This has not infrequently resulted in the creation of vast lakes, with resultant change of local weather patterns over certain areas.

147

The Canterbury Plains. (left)
The patchwork that is the Canterbury Plains is created by an heroic amount of sheer hard work — meticulously straight fencelines, the careful rotating of crop and pasture, and the dark lines of pine and macrocarpa windbreaks, planted to protect the light, silty topsoil from the boisterous nor'west winds.

Timaru Harbour and Wharves. (above)
The prodigious nineteenth century engineering, with horse and dray and wheelbarrow and pick and shovel, steam-winches and primitive explosives, that created a port out a shallow indentation in Canterbury's Pacific coast now provides an outlet point for the abundant produce of richly alluvial plains and the fertile, rolling hills of hinterland. Lyttelton, on Banks Peninsula, was always the principal Canterbury port; but in the days before the treacherous Rakaia and Rangitata Rivers were adequately bridged, men had to find another means of exporting seasonal produce. Timaru therefore became established as a port, and prospered.

Otago Peninsula. (over page)
An echo of old Scotland is in the dry-stone fences, the sheltering clumps of wind-sculpted trees, the occasional blaze of gorse and the tidy houses and barns, where Otago Peninsula lies alongside a harbour which is like a long and narrow loch. A mere stone's throw from the city of Dunedin, the peninsula is considered to be in it, but is not really of it, being a different world entirely from the busy city across the harbour.

Tobacco Harvesting, Motueka Valley, Nelson. (above)
In Nelson Province, which is northerly enough to ensure mild winters, the spurs of the ranges enclose the fertile Motueka Valley, making it a sheltered sun-trap which yields fine harvests of tobacco, (above), along with hops and fruit, which is harvested at the end of the district's long growing season. Few New Zealanders are fully aware of the ideal climate in this region. Although it is indeed in the South Island, it lies on a latitude not far removed from that of the Hawkes Bay fruitbowl; and with high ranges giving protection from the Tasman Seaboard weather, it enjoys an east coast climate.

Nelson, from Quebec Road. (above right)
Nelson nestles about the curve of its bay, with hills rising steeply at its back — a

thriving centre for the richly fertile valleys in the folds of the northern ranges.
Once— and perhaps still — a favourite retirement spot because of its gently warm climate, it is today a thriving and busy city, surrounded by an intriguing mix of modern industrial complexes and cottage industries.

Pine Forest, Whangamoa, Nelson. (below right)
Vast acreages of pine, regimentally aligned, clothe the slopes of the high hills of Nelson province, (right), providing timber and, incidentally, holding firmly together slopes which would otherwise erode massively. Pine chips from the region have become a significant export, contributing handsomely to the whole country's economy.

Alpine Night, Queenstown and Lake Wakatipu. (previous page left)

There are lights to twinkle across the Frankton Arm of Lake Wakatipu when the daylight fails and the frost chills the evening air in Queenstown, (above.) In Queenstown itself, for most of the year, are heard the languages and accents of almost every country in the world, as tourists flock here for the summer and autumn sightseeing, and in winter and early spring for the magnificent skiing.

Main Street, Arrowtown. (previous page below)

When autumn colours the avenue in Arrowtown, the cosy cottages built by the old gold-seekers of last century come into their own, being small, for easy heating, and touchingly home-like, the kind of cottages that everyone's Granny lived in.

The town was built by goldminers in the 'sixties of last century, and has altered little since then. Even the newer houses and holiday homes hereabouts seek out the sunny slopes and sheltered nooks of this snug shelf at the foot of the high ranges. The first-comers won more than 200lb (100kg) of gold in the first few weeks, in this vicinity.

Old Coaching Inn, Skippers Road, Queenstown. (previous page above)

The old inn remembers the days when the modern twenty-minute drive over good roads between Queenstown and Arrowtown was an arduous, punishing day's travel by pack-train or, later, two or three hours' journey by coach.

Queenstown, Lake Wakatipu and Walter Peak. (above left)

Lovely Queenstown is a garden built and flourishing upon what was once a tumble of rock, the terminal moraine of a glacier. A colourful town with a colourful past, it clusters down to its little, square bay and its miniature wharves as its former inhabitants used to do, as though still welcoming boatloads of gold prospectors arriving from Kingston, at the lake's southern end.

Arrow Basin, near Queenstown. (above)

Even the killing frosts of winter and the broiling suns of summer have not been able to prevent men from planting and cultivating and creating soft oases in the hard Arrow Basin country. As the gold-seekers crowded into these wild mountain valleys, farmers also came — not to gamble on finding fortunes in gold, but settling for the certainty that the miners would need food, and that farmers and farms would still be needed when all the gold had gone.

Otago Peninsula Rural Scene. (left)
The afternoon sun that touches the old
volcanic rim of Otago Peninsula lights a
scene of pastoral peace, where farms are
spread and sheep graze about the ancient,
towering lava plugs; for, like Lyttelton to
the north, Otago Harbour is a drowned
volcanic crater, in which ancient lava
spillings form reefs along its eastern shore.
The peninsula is almost parallel to the
mainland shore, forming the eastern wall
of a long, narrow harbour with one
winding, dredged, deep-water channel
which was contrived to bring ships to the
commercial heart of Dunedin.

Dunedin Sunrise. (below)
The early morning sun gilds the city of
Dunedin, built like Rome upon its seven
hills, across the harbour from the
Peninsula. The sun's first rays touch the
tops of the man-made towers, the high-rise
blocks on the university campus at the
northern end of the town. Otago settlers
built their city on land rejected by the
Canterbury colonists as being too rough,
hilly and densely forested.

*Acheron Accommodation House,
Marlborough. (above left)*

The early settlers found the tussock-
covered hills of Marlborough's high
country ideal for sheep. But for sheep
there had to be shepherds and drovers, and
for these there had to be shelter against
potential lethal high-country weather.
Accommodation houses were built, such
as this one at Acheron, near the head of
the Clarence River. In this virtually
treeless region, it had to be built of the
very ground on which it stands, of cob,
which is a puddled mixture of clay,
chopped tussock and chaff.

Hereford Cattle, Lake Hawea, Otago. (left)

Along the western shore of Lake Hawea,
beneath frowning peaks, a broad shelf of
land, (left), is a sheltered Shangri-la,
where fine Hereford cattle graze and grow
fat. On these "flats," in days gone by,
cereal crops have been grown, of such fine
quality that buyers were attracted from all
over the country.

Sheep, Lake Johnson, Otago. (above)

Near Lake Johnson, (above), sheep thrive
in a similar green and unexpected oasis.
Lake Johnson is a small lake near Lake
Hayes, in the Wakatipu Region. Its
principal claim to fame is the fine trout
fishing it affords, both brown and rainbow
trout being caught in its still and sheltered
waters. The lake's surroundings are not in
the least typical of the rugged Central
Otago landscape, being rolling green
downs, more typical of South Canterbury
or coastal Otago.

Benmore Hydro Dam and Lake. (above)
Forty years after Lake Mahinerangi was
formed, in an immensely larger
undertaking, engineers raised an earth
dam between two hills near Otematata,
behind which the Waitaki River backed
up to fill the twisting, deep valleys.
Benmore, (above), is one of the largest
earth dams in the world. It stands 110m
(360ft) high, 1,219m (4,000ft) long. Its lake
covers 8,300ha (32sq miles) with a
hundred miles of shoreline and 17 islands.
Its power output is 540,000kw, over 2,400
million units per year.

*Evening Light, Lake Mahinerangi, Otago.
(right)*
Where once a simple hill country stream
wriggled down through Waipori Gorge,
south of Dunedin, engineers in the early
years of this century built a dam, forming
an artificial lake to store water for the
Waipori Electric Power Stations. It was
named Mahinerangi, not after some
legendary Maori princess, but after the
daughter of Dunedin's (1911) Mayor.

Molesworth Cattle Drive, Marlborough. (above)

In the Marlborough highlands, on the broad, steep Molesworth Station, a summer cattle muster over the station's 460,000 mountainous acres begins a cattle drive along steep ridges, over wild river flats and down through the high passes to Culverden sale yards, where the mob is held, to be shipped by truck to Christchurch. Once divided into three vast sheep stations, the land was eaten out and burnt over too hard, too frequently. It became infested with rabbits, its hillsides eroded and the whole area seemingly ruined for livestock production. The Government took it over and it was gradually restored and stocked with cattle. Today it carries some 10,000 head, and serves as a research station for high-country farming.

Lake Tekapo Landscape, Mackenzie Country. (right)

The same fierce heat which scorches the Canterbury Plains is unrelieved over much of the Mackenzie Basin because of the sparsity of shade trees. But it ripens vast acreages of hay, to be mown and stored in huge, round bales, against the hungry winter. For at an altitude of over 700m (2,321ft), Lake Tekapo's climatic severity poses special problems in the maintenance of livestock in the cold months.

Sheep Leaving Yards, Canterbury. (above)
Many Canterbury runs were taken up by
Australian graziers, who brought with
them a better knowledge of farming in a
dry, drought-prone country than the
Englishmen possessed. But it was the
Englishmen who contrived to irrigate
some 2½-million acres with water-race
systems run from Canterbury's biggest
rivers, and increased the land's sheep-
carrying capacity dramatically. Today
close to 300,000 bales of wool are
produced annually in this area, and in
some years, over four million prime lamb
carceases are exported — a significant part
of New Zealand's overall earnings.

Harvesting, Canterbury Plains. (above left)
The patchwork of the Canterbury Plains
is composed of alternating fields of
pasture, fodder crops and cereal crops,
including barley, oats and wheat, with
sowings of winter feed for sheep, all
separated by fences which were originally,
(in that treeless expanse), raised as walls of
sods, on which were planted gorse hedges,
stockproof and dense enough to give
growing crops some measure of shelter.

South Canterbury Rural Scene. (left)
Where the hills begin to rise towards the
mountains, around the edges of the
Canterbury Plains, (left), pleasant rural
dales, hedged and green and shaded with
trees, contrast with the wilder hills
beyond. There tends to be a fairly sharp
demarcation between the rolling pastures
of the lower foothills, and the sudden

heights and bush-clad steeps of the sub-
alpine ranges. It is a contrast which
dramatically accentuates the ordered
neatness of those hills which man has
brought under cultivation.

*Pastoral Scene Near Waikari, North
Canterbury. (above)*
Waikari, Hawarden and Culverden are
three small communities set in a rolling,
upland basin walled about with high
ranges. Green and fertile, based on great
reefs of limestone, the countryside is ideal
for sheep, and the little townships bask in
the sunshine of long summers, and are
snugly sited and hospitable when the
high-altitude winters bring snow and
crackling frosts.

167

THE SOUTH ISLAND COAST

There is no particular or mystical quality about the Tasman Sea or the Pacific Ocean that would give a unique character to either of the coasts they have shaped along the flanks of this South Island. Both seas attack the shore with equal ferocity, or roll up to it in precisely the same kind of long swell, with a mighty threatening of surf where the continental shelf resists the inrushing water, or with a long, swift tidal rip where an off-shore current races around the turn of a headland and gouges an adjacent sweep of shore.

True, the Pacific coast has miles-long stretches of fine, sandy beach — but the Tasman coast has its Punakaiki, almost tropical under the caress of a warm current, with tall and graceful *nikau* palms, and the jungle-like bush coming down to the shore. True, the Tasman coast has its wild and rocky headlands — but the Pacific coast has its Kaikoura coast, with reef-guarded coves and romantically rock-bound capes and stern peninsulas at whose feet the bull kelp swirls and the incoming tides crash against granite cliffs.

It is the land, the magnificent, overpowering, high-reaching land that seems to marshall the sea and command its currents, deciding the shape of its own shores.

It's an ancient warfare, this battle between ocean and island. Here and there are traces of the sea's victory, as at the northern end of the island, where a network of drowned valleys forms the Marlborough Sounds where the defeated landscape has sunk into the water in a gigantic subsidence between Marlborough's seaward ranges and the distant coast of the South Taranaki Bight; or where the ocean has breached the walls of volcanic craters to form the harbours of Lyttelton, Akaroa and Dunedin. Here and there the land has been victorious, as where its rivers, bringing down gravel from the mountains, built up the Canterbury Plain until it reached out and snared the island which became Banks Peninsula.

In places, the coastline runs across the trend of the mountain ranges, to form a rugged shore deeply indented with bays and coves and land-locked havens, or deeply gashed with fiords. Elsewhere, the plains and coastward hills terminate abruptly in high cliffs, at whose base narrow shingle beaches are pounded by ocean rollers along a steeply shelving shore. And where rivers run out between sheltering headlands, beaches have built up —

Sunrise, Lyttelton Harbour.
The early sun, peeping over the rim of the drowned volcanic crater which forms Lyttelton Harbour wakens the small, pleasant, tree-shaded harbourside settlements that cluster about the walls of the ancient crater. Lyttelton Harbour was to have been the site of Canterbury's principal city, and was named in honour of Lord Lyttelton, the Chairman of the Canterbury Association. But the site proved to be too cramped and too short of fresh water, beneath those basalt walls.

Mitre Peak, Milford Sound. (previous page)

The massive peaks which wall Milford Sound rise sheer from the cold, clear water to heights of over 1,500m (5,000ft), and it is their prodigious height which makes the Sound seem narrow, though it is actually up to 5km (3 miles) wide.

The Otago Coast North of Taieri Mouth, Otago. (right)

The South Otago coast, north of Taieri Mouth, runs in successive crescents of sandy beach, swept clean by the current which, diverted from its southward course by Otago Peninsula, swings back inshore again at Brighton, until the out thrust hump of hilly land, bulging into the sea from Taieri Mouth, forces it seaward again.

Stewart Island, Viewed from Cosy Nook, Southland. (above)

Cosy Nook, (left), on the southern coast of the South Island, somewhat protected by the guardian rocks and reefs from boisterous Foveaux Strait, offers a view of distant Stewart Island, with its sharply conical Mount Anglem and its darkly forested ranges.

Ernest Island, Stewart Island. (above)
The South Arm of the magnificent Port Pegasus harbour on the south-eastern side of the main island is guarded from the ocean swell by a great hump of land indented with coves. Some idea may be obtained of the sudden violence of the seas in these parts when even on the lee side of this hump, anchorages have names like Disappointment Cove and Fright Cove. On the windward side, it is hardly suprising to find tiny Ernest Island, standing in the mouth of a long, deep inlet, marked on the charts as a 'small craft retreat." But Ernest Island itself is a peacefully idyllic knob of land, with its bird-loud bush, and a tree-fringed, curving bay on its own leeside.

handsome sweeps of sand backed, sometimes, by bush, and sometimes by dunes, pale blue-green with marram grass and lupins.

There are beaches that stand behind rocky reefs and gaze out across cold, southern waters towards the far, ice-bound seas of Antarctica, far beyond the rim of the horizon. There are beaches that are windswept and wild and strewn with driftwood. There are even beaches that are a rock-hound's delight, strewn with gemstones deposited by currents which tore them from frowning volcanic cliffs. There are beaches which sit at a city's feet, tidy, with barbered lawns behind them and a safe and gentle, sandy-bottomed bay lapping at them with gentle tides.

The character of the South Island's coastline is infinitely varied, abounding in inlets and indentations that make it a small-boat navigator's paradise. Rich in scenic variety, and dotted with natural wonders such as odd rock formations, blowholes, caves, cruel reefs, and the white smile of long curves of surf, it is never far from any New Zealander's door — and it is by no means the least of the South Island's magnificent scenic attractions.

Toko Mouth, South Otago. (below)
The Toko Stream meanders down to a
sandy coast through a reedy, scrub-patched
fen, to spill into a bay of calm beauty,
gently shelving and safe, where South
Otago people have built holiday homes to
which they bring their children for the
long summer holidays. The area contains
a special reserve known as Centennial
Park, an excellent camping ground. An
ocean current which sweeps along this
coast maintains a water temperature of
around 15.6°C (60°F) all year round.

*Coastal Cliffs Near Kaitangata, South
Otago. (right)*
South of Toko Mouth, the uprising land
stands above the Pacific Ocean atop tall
cliffs of crumbly-looking conglomerate
which, nevertheless, is as hard as concrete,
and is seamed, in the vicinity of
Kaitangata, with coal. The coast abounds
in fish, and several fleets of small fishing
boats operate just off shore, and have their
anchorages in river mouths and headland-
protected bays.

Southland Dawn, Riverton. (previous page)

At the western extremity of the sandy curve of bay between Invercargill's Oreti Beach and the township of Riverton, Howells Point thrusts eastward, a sheltering spearpoint of a headland, making the estuary of the Aparima and Pourakino Rivers a secure anchorage for fishing boats which operate in the stormy waters of Foveaux Strait.

Oamaru Harbour and Cape Wanbrow. (left)

Oamaru Harbour, (right), sheltered from the southerly winds by Cape Wanbrow, was once a busy coastal port. With the decline of coastal shipping, it has become a haven for a fishing fleet. The harbour and the town — occupy yet another ancient volcanic crater.

Karitane Coast, Otago. (right)

The Karitane Coast must be one of the most idyllic spots in New Zealand, with its curving, sandy, gently shelving beaches and its romantic peninsula, all backed by a story-book countryside of tidy, green farms. Here, too, small boats form an off-shore fishing fleet, anchoring, between fishing sweeps, in the shelter of the peninsula.

The Moeraki Boulders, North Otago. (left)

Moeraki Beach, on North Otago's coast, is strewn with round septarian stones, geological oddities which seem to have formed around a crystalline centre over aeons of time, much as a pearl forms around a piece of grit in an oyster shell. In Maori lore, the stones are sweet potatoes and gourds, the cargo of a wrecked ancestral canoe.

Punakaiki Seascape. (above)

The Tasman Sea coast can be wild, lonely and magnificently moody. The beach south of Punakaiki and north of Greymouth, (above), with its foaming breakers and its salt-laden haze is typical of much of the South Island's west coast scenery. A warm current just offshore transforms the coastal hills into a facsimile of tropical jungle in this area, even to the fringe of nikau palms that nod and sway above the beaches.

Early Morning Scene, East Coast of Stewart Island. (right)

Though Stewart Island possesses luxuriant forests, and coves and sandy beaches that seem to belong to a tropic isle, it still manages, in odd places and at certain times and in certain lights, to convey a reminder that it is, after all, a last outpost, the final dot of habitable land, between the main islands and the Antarctic.

The Pancake Rocks, Punakaiki. (left)

Close to the Porari Rivermouth beach, the same turbulent sea has pounded and gouged and carved a headland into a fantastic semblance of piles of great, grey pancakes, (above.) It is somewhat awe-inspiring, to stand on the ground in this vicinity and feel it tremble to the surge and suck of the sea in long caverns beneath your feet. Here and there, explosions of air compressed at the end of such caverns by the inrushing water have burst through the cavern roofs, forming blowholes through which great geysers of seawater jet high into the air.

Jackson Bay, South Westland. (above right)

Farther south, where the sea reaches almost to the feet of the Alps, its waters seem subdued, lapping gently at the narrow beaches as though overawed at last by the power of the mountains; though even here, storms can send the sea crashing right to the foot of the Jackson Bay cliffs. There is wharfage for coastal vessels here, and the bay has long been a minor port, though of much diminished importance now that roads from the north and the east reach Haast and the cattle runs in this "frontier" area.

Porari Rivermouth, Punakaiki Coast. (below right)

Where the Porari River tumbles down from the hills to the Punakaiki coast, and sweeps out across the sand through a gap in the rugged cliffs, the Tasman Sea has stood back and permitted a fine, sandy beach to establish itself. This part of the west coast is a favourite holiday spot, beautiful, sheltered by seaward-trending, high spurs. Its beaches are gently shelving and safe.

Tahunanui Beach, Nelson. (left)
Throughout Nelson's long, hot summers,
Tahunanui Beach, (left), on the shores of
Tasman Bay, is crowded with sunloving
humanity; but as evening closes in, the
oyster catchers and stilts and gulls reassert
their ancient ownership as they feed in the
wake of a receding tide.

*Tarakohe Coast,
Golden Bay, Nelson. (above)*
The marble hills of Takaka slope down to
the Tarakohe coast on the eastern shores
of Golden Bay, that rocky and often
spectacular seaboard. Abel Tasman, in
1642, called it "Murderers' Bay," because
Maoris attacked his ships' boats while they
were on a watering detail, and killed some
of his men. Today it is known as Golden
Bay, and its climate and deeply indented,
attractive coast are well described by such
a warm and pleasant title.

Picton, Marlborough Sounds. (above)
It is difficult to realise that Picton, spilling down the slopes from the foot of the bush-clad ranges, is the South Island terminal of the ferry link between the two islands. Once Wellington's rival as proposed seat of Government, the little town (population 3,430) at the head of Queen Charlotte Sound remains a tranquil holiday resort, linked to the workaday south by thin ribbons of road and rail through the protecting hills.

Maori Leap Caves, Kaikoura. (right)
The Maori Leap Caves, (left), near Kaikoura, in limestone cliffs once hammered by the sea, now stand well back from the shore, eerie caverns hung with stalactites dripping like spilled toffee, and hide in their dark corners the ancient bones of seal and penguin amongst the forgotten ocean flotsam of lime-encrusted driftwood and empty shells.

Kaikoura, East coast. (above)
The little town of Kaikoura spreads itself
casually in tiers above a steeply shelving,
shingly beach, its pleasant bay wrapped
protectively in the arms of rocky reef and
stubby peninsula. In the bay, seals fish
alongside men in the long ocean swell;
and over all leans the lofty Seaward
Kaikoura Range, presenting within one
small area a microcosmic view of the
essential South Island — mountain, forest,
farm and shore.

*Tennyson Inlet, Marlborough Sounds.
(above)*

Tennyson Inlet, (above), branching
southward from the landlocked waterway
known as Tawhitinui Beach, is typical of
the Marlborough Sounds — deep, well
sheltered and watched over by brown,
forest-patched hills, In this network of
waterways, a sizeable navy could anchor,
but most of the traffic upon these
sheltered reaches consists of pleasure boats
and the launches which serve otherwise
isolated farms.

*Okuri Bay & D'Urville Island,
Marlborough Sounds. (right)*

An ancient and cataclysmic subsidence
once plunged a landscape of dovetailing
spurs and high ridges deep beneath the
waters of the South Taranaki Bight. The
hills above Okuri ("Place of Dogs") Bay,
(right), and the rugged spurs of D'Urville
Island were once the peaks of continuous
ranges, now drowned beneath the blue
waters of French Pass.

Mt Shewell and Fitzroy Bay, Marlborough Sounds. (left)

Fitzroy Bay, (left), is a complex harbour with many coves and inlets. A long spur from Mount Shewell, 777m (2550ft), runs down to Sheep Point, northern head of the almost landlocked bay, and the hills, and the mountain itself, like most Marlborough Sounds countryside, is a sun-browned pasture grazed over by sheep, and patched with exotic and native forest.

Whariki Beach, Cape Farewell. (above)

Whariki Beach, (above) on the western side of Cape Farewell, looks out, past the off-shore rocks, across the stormy Tasman Sea. The region is known for its beautiful sunsets. Cape Farewell was the last land sighted by Captain James Cook as he departed from New Zealand after his first exploratory voyage around the coast, and set sail for Australia.

191

Kaikoura Coast. (above)

The Kaikoura Ranges run straight, parallel courses to the sea, and drop abruptly into its depths, to form a rugged, rock bound shore of jagged reefs and swirling kelp, (above), south of where the Clarence River pours out from its high, hanging valleys and spreads out across a boulder fan as it rushes down to the sea. Like England's Cornish coast, or the stormy coast of Maine, it is a place of deep little inlets where the crayfish, from which it gets its name, (Kaikoura means "Feast of Crayfish"), are still abundant.

First published in 1982 as two titles 'The Beauty of New Zealand's North Island' and 'The Beauty of New Zealand's South Island'. Reprinted in 1985 and 1987.

This combined edition first published in 1988 and reprinted 1989, 1990, 1991 (twice) and 1992.

Published by Kowhai Publishing Ltd
10 Peacock Street, Auckland
299 Moorhouse Avenue, Christchurch

Printed in Hong Kong

ISBN 0 908598–35–1